Contests of Initiative

CONTESTS OF INITIATIVE

*Countering China's Gray Zone Strategy
in the East and South China Seas*

by Raymond Kuo

SCHAR SCHOOL'S

Center for
Security Policy Studies
at George Mason University

December 2020

Westphalia Press
An Imprint of the Policy Studies Organization
Washington, DC

Westphalia Press
An imprint of Policy Studies Organization
1527 New Hampshire Ave., NW
Washington, D.C. 20036
info@ipsonet.org

ISBN: 978-1-63723-704-5

Cover and interior design by Jeffrey Barnes
jbarnesbook.design

Daniel Gutierrez-Sandoval, Executive Director
PSO and Westphalia Press

Updated material and comments on this edition
can be found at the Westphalia Press website:
www.westphaliapress.org

ACKNOWLEDGEMENTS

Working on Asian security policy while being Taiwanese American is an exercise in moral dissonance. You must value two contradictory imperatives at the same time. There is the democratic injunction for greater international recognition, respect, and sovereignty for Taiwan, born of the country's political, cultural, social, and economic vibrancy. But there is the accompanying dread that taking even small steps towards this goal—let alone achieving it—would cost thousands of American and Taiwanese lives and endanger millions more for a deeply uncertain outcome. No matter what analytical conclusions you reach, one half of you suffers, perhaps even both.

But this dissonance can no longer be avoided. China's assertiveness and provocations undermine Asian security, and there is increasing American recognition that engagement has failed and that we must now turn to peer competition. This is the central challenge of small regional states: how to survive within the strategic environment created by intensifying US-China contestation. For the US, how can it marshal Asian antipathy to Chinese military and foreign policies and create lasting leadership?

I hope this project provides the actionable analysis and policy recommendations that can successfully resolve this dissonance. Any failures in this endeavor are solely mine.

This book would never have been published without Ellen Laipson and Michael A. Hunzeker of the Center for Security Policy Studies at George Mason University's Schar School of Policy and Government. Thank you both for all your help and guidance.

The Strategic Studies Institute at the U.S. Army War College provided financial support for this book through its External Research Associates Program. A special thanks to Diane Chido of DC Analytics for her help in securing that funding and during the research process. I am grateful to Daniel Gutierrez-Sandoval and Rahima Schwenkbeck of the Policy Studies Organization for shepherding this book through production and publication.

Finally, this book is dedicated to my parents, Kuonan and Sue Kuo. They too had to navigate that same moral dissonance: first as Taiwanese immigrants, then as American citizens. Thank you for instilling in me a love of both my homes.

TABLE OF CONTENTS

FOREWORD

I am pleased to present *Contests of Initiative: Countering China's Gray Zone Strategy in the East and South China Seas,* by Raymond Kuo. Kuo is a political scientist with deep expertise in East Asian security issues. His study explores the current dynamics in the East and South China Seas, positing an increasingly ambitious China against the prevailing role of the United States as a security provider in this critical region. Kuo offers an original and compelling set of policy responses for the United States and its allies to China's gray zone strategy in the region, those coercive measures short of war that appear to dominate Beijing's approach in its immediate maritime area.

The study will be of great value to those in the national security community with responsibility for US policies in East Asia, but it also provides important insights for strategic planners and analysts who will be grappling with the larger strategic dimensions of US-China relations, certain to be the paramount issue in global politics for the foreseeable future.

This fine study is the third in a series edited by the Center for Security Policy Studies at the Schar School of Policy and Government at George Mason University. You may also find the earlier titles in this occasional series of interest:

- *#1 Terrorism Vanquished: The Italian Approach to Defeating Terror,* by Simon Clark (September 2018)
- *#2 A Question of Time: Enhancing Taiwan's Conventional Deterrence Posture,* by Michael Hunzeker and Alexander Lanoszka (November 2018)

We are pleased to partner with the Policy Studies Organization, which is publishing this series, *International Security Challenges.* We intend to explore a wide range of international security topics in future studies, from technological and doctrinal aspects of conflict and war, to regional and transnational issues that profoundly affect the security of states and societies, without necessarily engaging military force. Our studies are also opportunities for Schar School scholars to collaborate with other security scholars and policy practitioners.

The Center for Security Policy Studies also offers virtual and in-person programs and activities, and features writings by Schar School graduate students and faculty. For more on CSPS, please visit csps.gmu.edu.

Ellen Laipson

Director, Center for Security Policy Studies
Editor, International Security Challenges Series
Schar School of Policy and Government
George Mason University

December 2020

EXECUTIVE SUMMARY

Since 2010, China has launched a wide-ranging assertion of sovereignty over nearly all of the East and South China Seas. Its paramilitary naval forces drive off vessels from ten rival claimants to assert control and seize territory. President Xi Jinping appears to have elevated this maritime sovereignty issue to a "core interest," equal in importance to the People's Republic's longstanding positions on Taiwan, Tibet, and Xinjiang.[1] This promises to intensify regional maritime conflicts and may even have presaged recent flare-ups in territorial disputes with India and Bhutan.

In the Seas, China employs a "gray zone" strategy, using coercive power to solidify and normalize its control while simultaneously preventing military escalation. Beijing relies on paramilitary units—the Chinese Coast Guard (CCG) and the People's Armed Forces Maritime Militia (PAFMM)—for this strategy. Backed by the People's Liberation Army Navy (PLAN), these forces escalate minor actions by regional states, flood the conflict area with vessels, drive off rival vessels, and enforce compliance with Beijing's sovereignty claims. Guarded by these units, China has dredged over 3,200 acres of land since 2013 to create new outposts around disputed marine features. Many of these outposts now host military installations that support blockades of territory claimed and administered by US partners and that assist operations to harass these countries' commercial and even military vessels, further bolstering Beijing's control. Regional states have protested these actions, but generally cannot confront Chinese activities without escalating to direct military force.

Secretary of State Mike Pompeo (2020) recently articulated US aims in

---

1   The Philippines submitted an arbitration case to the UN Convention on the Law of the Sea to adjudicate territorial disputes between Manila and Beijing. In response, in 2013, Xi declared China "absolutely will not give up its legitimate rights, much less sacrifice its national core interests," suggesting that at least Xi grants these maritime disputes the same stature as other central security interests. (See https://www.brookings.edu/articles/xi-jinping-and-chinas-maritime-policy/.)

In addition, China's 2015 National Security Law appears to have expanded this position into national policy. Article 11 declares that "The sovereignty and territorial integrity of China shall not be infringed upon or partitioned," and it charges the CCP generally and the National Security Commission (headed by Xi) specifically with this responsibility. (See http://eng.mod.gov.cn/publications/2017-03/03/content_4774229.htm.)

these conflicts: "to preserve peace and stability, uphold freedom of the seas in a manner consistent with international law, maintain the unimpeded flow of commerce, and oppose any attempt to use coercion or force to settle disputes."[2] China's territorial aggression and changes to the status quo directly challenge American interests. Washington regularly conducts Freedom of Navigation Operations (FONOPs) to contest Beijing's actions, but these have failed to prevent continued island and installation building, coercion against regional states, and even near-collisions with US naval forces.

To develop an effective response, this book conceptualizes gray zone strategies as "contests of initiative" that rest on two pillars. First, an adversary must possess escalation dominance, the ability to defeat local states on multiple rungs of the escalation ladder. With this, it can rely on the threat of superior conventional power to deter wider retaliation, while using sub-conventional forces to seize territory, exert control and compliance, and—critically— keep disputes below the level inviting a global power's engagement. Unless targets develop similar forces, they must rely on either military escalation —often economically and politically costly—or concede. Second, regional political fragmentation allows belligerents to more easily isolate or co-opt resisting states. This also raises the costs, coherence of regional political support, and uncertainty of outcomes for, say, US intervention.

Washington and its Asian partners must address both pillars to defeat China's gray zone challenge. This book outlines three possible courses of action:

1. *Accommodation*: Washington accedes to China's understanding of its maritime territorial claims in exchange for Beijing's adherence to international rules regarding freedom of navigation.

2. *Renewed Pivotal Deterrence*: The US unilaterally develops and deploys paramilitary capabilities to meet China's forces symmetrically, while simultaneously preventing other states from once again launching their own territorial revisions.

3. *Extended Deterrence*: Washington fosters a political settlement to regional maritime disputes and enhances military coordination with its allies to confront Chinese actions.

---

2   Pompeo is reiterating US strategic objectives originally set in US Department of Defense (2015, 1).

China responds to and is deterred by allied coordination threatening American intervention and military escalation. The last option therefore offers the best chance to protect and advance US interests in the East and South China Seas. However, it constitutes a substantial increase in Washington's security commitment and political engagement in Asia.

Balancing US leadership against these costs is ultimately a political question. China's assertions present Washington with a critical opportunity to decisively settle Asia's maritime sovereignty problems. America can lock-in long-term regional leadership through the proposed international institutions, but only if it possesses a clear understanding of gray zone dynamics, extended deterrence's benefits for local partners, and how this strategy increases the risk of military confrontation to achieve lasting security.

CHAPTER 1

CONTESTS OF INITIATIVE

Introduction

The 2015 National Defense Authorization Act's (NDAA) Asia-Pacific Maritime Security Strategy articulates three strategic objectives for Asia's maritime zones:

1. To safeguard the freedom of the seas;

2. To deter conflict and coercion; and

3. To promote adherence to international law and standards. (US Department of Defense 2015, 1)

China's gray zone strategy obstructs these goals and challenges the prevailing maritime order, embodied in the UN Convention on the Law of the Sea (UNCLOS). Beijing claims that "historic rights"—especially the "Nine-Dash Line"—entitle it to 90 percent of the South China Sea and stretches of the East China Sea. This area extends as much as 1,200 miles away from Mainland China and overlaps with rival claims from ten other countries. Since 2013, Beijing has created over 3,200 acres of land around maritime rocks and features and has significantly expanded already existing installations. Many of these have been equipped with military early warning, support, and strike facilities. Despite protests from rival claimants, China enforces its control through a "gray zone" strategy relying on paramilitary forces: the CCG—most armed with water cannons and light weapons—and the PAFMM, whose most advanced vessels are similarly armed (US Department of Defense 2020, 72; see also Erickson 2017; Kennedy and Erickson 2016). Units from these commands form swarms of nominally "civilian," not-heavily-armed ships willing to ram other vessels to drive them off, enforce compliance with territorial sovereignty claims, and normalize Chinese dominance in the East and South China Seas. Regional states lack the forces to meet this challenge symmetrically, while the PLAN's growing capabilities dissuade escalation to conventional military conflict. In short, China possesses local escalation dominance, leaving regional countries with few strategic, operational, or tactical options.

This book joins recent analyses attempting to understand and develop US and allied responses to gray zone challenges. It presents three courses of action Washington can take to achieve its strategic objectives: accommodation with China, pivotal deterrence dissuading revisionism from any country, and extended deterrence drawing East and Southeast Asian security partners into a comprehensive territorial settlement. Each option has its own set of assumptions, risks, and costs, reflecting different ways to resolve the challenges posed by gray zone strategies.

This chapter begins by defining the gray zone as a strategy, how states organize resources and capabilities according to specific decision-making frameworks to achieve national goals. Following Lanoszka (2016) and Mazarr (2015), moderately revisionist states use this approach to upend parts of the regional order, but preserve others. By keeping provocations below the conventional thresholds of war, they can delay, disrupt, or deny effective and cost-effective responses from other states. Gray zone strategies are "contests of initiative." Once control (whether over territory or by achieving policy compliance) has been established, it is much harder to reverse. As a result, moderate revisionists have incentives to seize objectives first, imposing *fait accompli* on reluctant responders. Two factors are especially important to capturing and maintaining the initiative. The first is a revisionist's coercive capabilities, particularly the ability to defeat targets at multiple escalation levels. With this "escalation dominance," revisionists use paramilitary forces to achieve their goals, while conventional power deters retaliation. Conflicts are restricted to domains where challengers can press their unmatched advantages and where targets must suffer unacceptable costs to respond. This dynamic is particularly effective against politically and diplomatically isolated targets. Consequently, the second factor is the degree of regional security cohesion/fragmentation. The greater the fragmentation, the more easily a revisionist can isolate a state, leverage its escalation dominance, and prevent responses by third parties. Alliances are critical to closing these security gaps and bolstering political cohesion among Asian maritime countries.

The Gray Zone as Strategy

This book follows Lanoszka (2016) in defining the "gray zone" as a strategy of political coercion through the use of military, paramilitary, unconventional, and/or irregular capabilities. States pursuing this strategy coerce targets into complying with their preferred policies, but without the overt use of conventional military force. Mazarr (2015) notes that moderate revisionists disproportionately use this approach. These countries fall in between status quo-oriented countries on the one hand and "predatory" states seeking to overturn the international order on the other. Status quo-oriented states are satisfied with the distribution of benefits they receive from the international system, whether that be acceptable borders, their level of economic interdependence, or status within international institutions. These countries have little reason to launch coercive challenges to the prevailing order. On the other side, Mazarr calls certain states like North Korea or Nazi Germany "predators" that seek significant changes to their status and position within the system. These can include pushes for territorial acquisition, revising international norms and rules, gaining a greater share of interstate economic exchange, and recognition of their prerogatives and control over spheres of influence.

Moderate revisionists fall between these two points. They benefit from certain elements of the global order, such as norms against military conflict and an open trade system. But they are dissatisfied with others, seeking "to remold, shape, and modify [these elements] to enhance their own standing" (Mazarr 2015, 21). But these efforts and objectives are limited, for two reasons. First, while these states hope to achieve specific policy changes, they do not want to endanger the benefits derived from the order. Revisionism on security issues, for example, must be limited and its effects constrained to avoid unacceptable costs to, say, inward financial flows from the open international economic system. Indeed, Mazarr notes that moderate revisionists can be essential supporters of parts of the global order, complicating status quo states' response. The revisionist can leverage its critical position within, say, the free trade system to exert pressure on target states. Alternatively, it can exchange compliance with rules in one area for concessions in another (Poast 2013), forcing other countries into policy tradeoffs or reducing third party support for a target's position.

Second, moderate revisionists are (almost by definition) both stronger than many other states and weaker than some, whether individually or collectively. The revisionist possesses escalation dominance: the ability to "engage and defeat its target at different levels of military escalation" (Lanoszka 2016, 178), whether conventional military, paramilitary (e.g., coast guards), cyber warfare, etc. However, this dominance only applies "locally": while the belligerent can defeat, say, individual neighbors, it fears retaliation from more powerful states or coalitions of states. It lacks "global" escalation dominance, as Lanoszka (2016) discusses:

More direct use of force might elicit resistance from a militarily superior coalition of adversaries. If the target has powerful allies or friends, then hybrid warfare also helps avoid triggering an intervention that the belligerent does not believe it can handle. (180)

Consequently, gray zone strategies direct sufficient coercive power against local, individually weaker targets to secure compliance with the belligerent's policies. However, those efforts are simultaneously limited or designed to avoid retaliation by stronger, often extra-regional states.[3]

---

3 Articulating what this book does *not* consider part of the gray zone will sharpen its definition. Numerous scholars have written on this concept and on the related ones of "hybrid warfare," "unconventional warfare," and even guerilla warfare and insurgency. Across all these concepts, analysts gather together traditionally disparate approaches to or domains of political violence and conflict. Murray and Mansoor (2012) define hybrid warfare as "a conflict involving a combination of conventional military forces and irregulars (guerrillas, insurgents and terrorists), which could include both state and non-state actors, aimed at achieving a common political purpose" (3). Glenn (2009) and Hoffman (2012) both include criminal and terrorist behavior in their definitions, alongside the simultaneous use of conventional weapons and irregular tactics. Mazarr (2015) emphasizes the use of similar tools in the gray zone. The difference is chiefly in the intensity of violence used, although a clear dividing line is not articulated (nor perhaps is it possible or analytically necessary to do so). Marine Lt. Col. Bill Nemeth similarly highlights how militants transition easily between conventional and guerrilla tactics and terrorism under his definition, choosing the approach best suited to their immediate operational and tactical conditions (Nemeth 2002). Yet Echevarria (2016) also highlights the fluidity of these boundaries and the flexibility it affords practitioners. Indeed, he uses "hybrid" and "gray zone" interchangeably.

All these studies must work out how the conventional and unconventional components interrelate in an analytically coherent and useful manner. This is challenging. The interaction must be sufficiently broad to ensure that the concept applies to a meaningful number of cases, but be narrow enough to be conceptually useful. Typically in assessing the gray zone, these definitions focus on the "irregular" component, contrasting it with an ideal type of conventional warfare as clear in attribution (i.e., who is doing the fighting), rapidly achieved so as to be decisive (i.e., how quickly do they want to achieve their goals), and destructive in orientation (i.e., how they want to go about it). Conventional warfare is conceived as one of "brute force," focused on a target's capitulation, while the unconventional component is coercive, attempting to achieve the target's political compliance.

But as Lanoszka (2016) points out, this is a questionable analytical distinction. Nearly every war has featured combinations of conventional and irregular combat, criminal behavior, and adherence to formal rules of war. All conflicts feature characteristics often associated with unconventional war, including attributive deniability,

This tension between local and global escalation dominance drives other characteristics that analysts associate with gray zone strategies: attributive deniability, gradualism, and calibration to potential responses. For example, most gray zone definitions focus on thresholds: belligerents keep their actions below the level triggering a concerted response (Kapusta 2015; Mazarr 2015, 1; USSOCOM). This is because they lack global escalation dominance. But by possessing local dominance, particularly in sub-conventional capabilities, revisionists force targets into a quandary. Should the targets use more expensive, escalatory tools, including military force, to reinstate the status quo ante? How cost-effective would this be, particularly for a secondary interest and without overt military provocation by the revisionist state? Ideally for the revisionist, the calibration of paramilitary and military coercive power allows it to take advantage of established thresholds to achieve desired changes to the status quo while avoiding wider retaliation.

Similarly, revisionists can use ambiguous attribution to delay responses and widen commitment gaps between weaker and more powerful partners. For example, Cormac and Aldrich (2018)—building on Carson (2016), Carson and Yarhi-Milo (2017), Yarhi-Milo (2013), and others—highlight the role of "implausible" deniability. Challengers use these "open secrets" to coerce weaker states, but provide them or third-parties a possible rationale to avoid engagement or escalation. Ambiguity and debate about "what actually happened" slow allied decision-making and collective response, giving challengers windows to seize further objectives. This approach typifies recent Russian gray zone operations (Carson 2016a; Carson et al. 2017; Cormac and Aldrich 2018; Yarhi-Milo 2013). "Little green men" appeared in Crimea and Ukraine during the 2014 crises, intensifying ethnic Russian grievances, fomenting disturbances, and creating what Russia claimed were

---

gradualism, and calibration of goals and actions to avoid specific types of retaliatory responses.

This book makes two points cutting through this confusion. First, it follows Lanoszka (2016) in arguing that the "unconventional" characteristics of gray zone strategies flows from the practitioner's local escalation dominance but global weakness. Such actors are simultaneously triangulating against both weaker and stronger opponents. Second, it follows Mazarr in highlighting that gray zone strategies are not weapons of the weak, but tools of moderate or even powerful actors. These states deliberately choose *not* to directly utilize all dimensions of their power, reserving the threat of vertical or horizontal escalation to address specific vulnerabilities and shape adversary behavior.

spontaneously formed "self-defense groups." These groups then captured important transportation and logistics hubs. This both facilitated and justified Moscow's subsequent conventional military intervention as a humanitarian mission. Putin later admitted the "little green men" were indeed Russian Special Operations Forces (Borger 2014; Lally 2014). By that point, however, this ambiguity increased European reluctance to intervene, giving Moscow time to create additional facts on the ground that further complicated third party responses (see Hunzeker and Lanoszka 2018). Moreover, as Carson (2016) and Yarhi-Milo (2013) discuss, such secrecy can convey resolution and intention. Belligerents demonstrate their willingness to risk exposure of a "secret" activity to obtain their objectives. They also provide targets with a face-saving option to decline engagement or escalation. In short, deniability delays, deters, or otherwise complicates an adversary's response, providing revisionists the time and political space to seize objectives and solidify control.

Note, however, that deniability may be useful in campaigns to establish control over territory, but is less helpful in achieving policy compliance. Put another way, ambiguous attribution can support strategies of denial, where seizure of territory is the underlying objective. Opponents need not consent nor cooperate for the strategy to be successful, although that would reduce costs. By contrast, if a revisionist desires compliance with its preferred rules, target countries must know whose forces are making the demands to know which rules to follow. The opponent's consent is necessary for success. Even if targets internalize and accept a revisionist's domination, the latter must still credibly promise and impose costly retaliation for egregious or prominent challenges to its rules. Ambiguity contradicts this strategy of punishment, which relies on clearly delineated guidelines, punishments, and responsible parties (Altman 2017).

Whether pursuing a strategy of denial or punishment, success hinges more on the revisionist's coercive capabilities, rather than the target's defensive means. Indeed, gray zone practitioners develop and select forces and capabilities specifically to sidestep a defender's preferred political and military responses. This better avoids retaliation by stronger states, often—but not invariably—producing "strategic gradualism." Conventional operations are attractive because they can rapidly settle a dispute. But they risk a much quicker and broader response from status quo states. Under these conditions, the moderate revisionist's position within the international order becomes a liability. Military acquisition of territory, for example, is a clear violation of the order's rules and incites broad condemnation as a result. Belligerents become a "predatory" state, opening them up to cross-domain punishments like financial controls, political and economic sanctions, and closer security cooperation from a broader array of status quo countries. To avoid this, moderate revisionists can use slower, and possibly less effective, means to achieve their goals. Subterfuge and espionage require medium- and even long-term patience before their benefits emerge. As Gilli and Gilli (2016) demonstrate, belligerents must also create the systems to put such information to effective use once it has been extracted. Fifth columns or propaganda spread slowly through a population, particularly if targeted states implement their own measures to blunt such actions. But they can prevent a militarized response by targets while eventually accomplishing the challenger's objectives. Even when pursuing more militarily aggressive gray zone strategies, revisionists typically use "salami tactics," slowing changing the "facts on the ground" to eventually present a *fait accompli* to status quo states (Altman 2017; Hunzeker and Lanoszka 2018; Mitchell and Grygiel 2014).

Note, however, that gray zone strategies need not be gradual. Russia seized Crimea and infiltrated eastern Ukraine in a matter of weeks. Strategic gradualism is more useful the larger the gap between local and global escalation dominance. A large gap implies more powerful outside actors who can intervene against revisionists with greater effectiveness and frequency. By contrast, with a smaller gap, more powerful belligerents can rely on faster, more disruptive methods to decisively settle disputes, trusting their capabilities at higher levels of escalation to deter militarized responses even against powerful states.

Contests of Initiative

The gap between local and global escalation dominance drives gray zone strategies. So what affects that gap? Put differently, *what factors determine whether a state adopts a gray zone strategy and makes a moderately revisionist challenge?* I argue that gray zone strategies are fundamentally "contests of initiative." There is an advantage to moving first instead of reacting, and continually pressing opponents to extract maximum concessions until the gray zone strategy's objectives are met. In short, conflicts of this type favor those states that can seize and maintain the initiative, defined as "the power of making our adversary's movements conform to our own" (Cherry 1921) or alternatively, "setting and dictating the terms of action" (Headquarters

2011). The Appendix provides statistical analysis justifying this conceptualization. Assessing all countries from 1979 to 2001, it identifies two factors—the coercive and the cohesive—systematically determining whether states launch revisionist challenges.

For the first factor, moderate revisionists must actually possess local escalation dominance. To reiterate, sub-conventional force is used to achieve the revisionist's objectives, while conventional power deters stronger retaliation. Conflict is therefore contained, kept within domains where challengers have unmatched advantages and where targets suffer unacceptable costs for military escalation. Local states are forced into an unenviable policy choice, where compliance and escalation are both undesirable. The coercive capabilities used in a gray zone strategy are subject to three conditions. First, their use must not by themselves draw in more powerful countries, either by their very nature or according to international norms. Nuclear weapons, for example, automatically attract great power engagement, as do certain ballistic missile systems and the weaponization of space. Moderate revisionists explicitly seek to avoid such engagement, the better to preserve the other order benefits they receive and prevent retaliation from a more powerful state. Instead, sub-conventional forces can more effectively exploit differences in interest intensity between local targets and global powers, and therefore local and global escalation dominance. These forces can elide a local target's military while avoiding the erosion of norms or regional instability that would invite a global power's entry. In essence, using paramilitary units, for example, potentially provides global powers a reason *not* to intervene in a dispute of secondary interest. Second, the revisionist's capabilities must be cost-effective on a *relative* basis. That is, the cost for belligerents to use sub-conventional forces must be lower than the cost for targets to respond. Seizing territory or enforcing policy compliance is relatively cheap, while rolling back those gains requires escalation that is more costly and difficult for status quo respondents. When this is the case, initiators enjoy a first-mover advantage until costs are (at least) equalized. Third, local escalation dominance also implies that the target's military power is largely irrelevant to gray zone contests.[4] Unless targets develop symmetrical capabilities (in the China case, this would be paramilitary forces equivalent in strength and quantity to the CCG and PAFMM), revisionists can

---

4   The Appendix's statistical analysis also tests for and validates this "null" point/finding.

simply deny engagement except in their preferred domain, steadily altering the status quo to their advantage.

For the second factor, initiative benefits from political fragmentation and a lack of coordination among local and global status quo states over the issue(s) being contested.[5] Interests of secondary importance for the more powerful status quo states, but of primary concern for local ones, are ideal for this strategy. The greater the divergence in interest alignment and intensity, the easier it is for a challenger to decouple powerful states from supporting the weaker ones' policies. Gray zone strategies attack the "seams" of the international order: those issue domains and geographic areas where the robustness, institutionalization, and formalization of interstate agreement are thinnest. Greater fragmentation also facilitates a challenger's ability to induce target states to support its control, dominance, or preferred foreign policies. These countries cannot rely upon outside support, and so may adhere to any rules, even disadvantageous ones, rather than risk punishment. Thus, "disordered" parts of the international system—regions or issues over which great powers or hegemons have not established clear rules or expressed a manifest interest in supporting—are particularly likely to receive gray zone incursions, as revisionists contest prevailing rules and shift control to their advantage (Litwak 2012).

This produces a somewhat paradoxical conclusion. Many analysts argue that greater operational and tactical flexibility is necessary to effectively confront gray zone strategies. This can include acquiring new weapons systems; asymmetric responses using economic and diplomatic levers; and more choices over when, how, and where to respond. Under these recommendations, the global power (the US) reserves the freedom of action generated by these new tools. But these options elide the political nature of gray zone challenges that target differences in interest intensity. Unless these measures are relatively cost-effective (i.e. they cost less for the status quo state to implement than for the revisionist to maintain), belligerents will eventually impose costs that outweigh the global power's interest in the dispute. Closing these political gaps requires less, not more, flexibility (see Ikenberry 2001; Schroeder 1976).[6] Formal alliances featuring robust coor-

---

5   For more on conflicts between primary and secondary interests among allies, see Cesa (2010).

6   Work on alliance abandonment makes a similar point (Beckley 2015; Benson 2012; Kim 2011).

dinating mechanisms generally reduce policy latitude and choice. But according to the statistical analysis, they are the factor that most consistently deters revisionist challenges. Rather than meet ambiguity with further ambiguity, status quo actors are better served by solidifying their security relations and responses through more extensive and comprehensive coordination. While alliances are slower and more constrained in decision-making than unilateral exercises of power, they foreclose the political gaps between global and local status quo states that gray zone challenges exploit.

Conclusion

In sum, this chapter defines the "gray zone" as a strategy. A moderately revisionist state seeks changes to some global rules or settlements. It uses dominant irregular forces, backed by the threat of superior conventional power, to extract concessions from weaker neighbors and simultaneously to deter, disrupt, or otherwise delay engagement by more powerful global states. This tension between the local and global produces the gray zone characteristics identified by previous analysis: probing redlines and thresholds, incremental changes through salami slicing tactics, plausible and implausible deniability, and strategic gradualism. From this definition, this book conceptualizes gray zone confrontations as contests of initiative. Once policy compliance is achieved or territory successfully seized, respondents face higher costs to escalate or wrest back control. Belligerents benefit from moving first and forcing others to respond.

This simple model of initiative focuses our inquiry on two factors: the revisionist's escalation dominance and the respondents' political cohesion/ fragmentation. The following chapter tracks these factors across China's gray zone strategy in the East and South China Seas from 2010–2015. Over the past two decades, Beijing has rapidly increased its conventional military capabilities. But it has simultaneously upgraded its "civilian" maritime forces, especially the CCG and PAFMM. This grants it local escalation dominance and the ability to coerce regional rivals below the threshold of conventional war. While Chinese assertiveness is creating a security backlash in Asia, two factors inhibit political cohesion among targets. First, the US policy of "pivotal deterrence"—seeking to prevent conflict escalation from all parties—has created ambiguity about Washington's intentions and preferred end-goals. The second factor—the lack of a comprehensive maritime settlement, typified by American excuses to avoid UNCLOS accession—exacerbates this. Without that strategic clarity, regional states cannot respond more assertively to Beijing's unilateral changes to the maritime status quo.

Based on that case analysis, the final chapter presents three policy options for the US to manage China's gray zone strategy and accomplish its regional security objectives. These are:

1. *Accommodation,* where Washington accedes to China's understanding of its maritime territorial claims in exchange for Beijing's adherence to international rules regarding freedom of navigation;

2. *Renewed pivotal deterrence,* where the US unilaterally develops and deploys sub-military capabilities to meet China's forces symmetrically and also deter other regional states from once again launching their own territorial revisions; and

3. *Extended Deterrence*: Washington fosters a political settlement to regional maritime disputes and enhances military coordination with its allies to confront Chinese actions.

Each option presents individuated and sometimes mutually exclusive recommendations. Which strategy the US chooses depends on its preferred level of security engagement, risk tolerance, and cost acceptance. Washington ultimately faces a political question: how much are the benefits of regional maritime stability and security worth, particularly when compared to other demands on limited military, political, and economic resources? This book cannot answer that fundamental question. Instead, it examines how changes to the East and South China Seas strategic environment force the US to alter its current strategy to meet its security goals.

CHAPTER 2

CHINA'S MARITIME GRAY ZONE STRATEGY, 2010–2015

Introduction

The previous chapter and the statistical appendix establish the coercive and cohesive determinants of gray zone strategies. This chapter applies that lens to East and Southeast Asia's maritime areas, examining how three elements shape China's gray zone strategy:

1. *Extensive Chinese Coercive Capabilities:* Beijing has local escalation dominance, possessing coercive forces that are numerically and in some cases qualitatively superior to its neighbors in multiple conflict domains. Its advantage in paramilitary forces is particularly pronounced, and regional states struggle to monitor and deter so many units using their own capabilities.

2. *US Pivotal Deterrence Strategy:* Washington has traditionally cultivated ambiguity about the extent and coverage of its regional alliance commitments to deter conflict by both China and its security partners (see Crawford 2003; Hsu 2010; Pan 2003; Pinsker 2003). While this strategy has succeeded in the past, shifts in allied intentions and a loss of power preponderance allow Beijing to probe and exploit American vagueness.

3. *Lack of Political Support and Consensus Regarding Asia's Maritime Settlement:* Regional fragmentation over UNCLOS definitions and comprehensiveness—coupled with lukewarm US support for the convention—means there is no focal institution local countries can uphold as a standard for conduct. China can more easily subvert challenges to its maritime operations and preferences, exploiting differences in Asian policy preferences to block collective responses and isolate actors.

Each enhances Beijing's ability to contest and control Asia's maritime zones. To demonstrate this, this chapter highlights evidence from five maritime disputes, briefly summarized in Table 1.[7] In total, these cases adhere to the "contests of initiative" logic. Allied coordination inviting US inter-

---

7   Readers are referred to Green et al. (2017) for more comprehensive accounts.

vention halts Chinese activities based on its local escalation dominance. This analysis will provide actionable guidance for the three courses of action presented in the next chapter.

Table 1: Summary of Key Cases

	Senkaku Trawler Collision	Scarborough Reef Standoff	Senkaku Nationalization Crisis	Second Thomas Shoal Standoff	Oil Rig Standoff
Year	2010	2012	2012	2013	2014
Target	Japan	The Philippines	Japan	The Philippines	Vietnam
Outcome	Chinese success: Fisherman returned	Chinese success: territory held by China	Partial Japanese success: administrative control retained. Partial Chinese success: normalized CCG incursions into territorial sea	Philippine success: retained control and resupplied outpost	Ambiguous: China completed most operations, but may have been driven off early

Case Selection

The Chinese government is famously secretive about its national security and foreign policy deliberations. This book consequently relies on non-Chinese sources and reports from Western and Asian think tanks, respected news agencies, and independent analysts. This could potentially skew the analysis, as it is impossible to determine whether these sources accurately reflect the Chinese leadership's thinking, incentives, and decisions. However, exploring multiple cases helps address this problem. If we can reliably establish the same fact patterns across each case, this should increase the reliability of our "contests of initiative" framing. Case selection also focuses the analysis. All five conflicts occurred within four years of each other and within the same phase of Chinese military modernization. This chapter therefore assesses analogous cases where Beijing deployed similar paramilitary units and platforms to conflict zones. Each dispute also concerns a vital Chinese interest. Beijing explicitly declared four cases to be "core" interests: the Scarborough Shoal standoff, the Second Thomas Shoal incident, the 2014 oil rig standoff, and potentially the 2010 trawler collision. In doing so, the Chinese Communist Party (CCP) signals that it treats these conflicts as politically equivalent to Taiwan, Tibet, and Xinjiang. In the middle of the remaining case—Japan's nationalization of the Senkaku Islands—the Chinese Foreign Ministry spokesperson responded to a question by stating, "the Diaoyu Islands are about sovereignty and territorial integrity. Of course, it's China's core interest" (Japan Times 2013). That language was later softened (see Campbell et al. 2013, 5), but Chinese paramilitary forces were deployed and operated in a similar manner as in the other cases. Finally, the heads of state of Vietnam, the US, and the Philippines remained the same throughout this period. This should cull the influence of alternative explanations and isolate the within-case impact of changes in escalation dominance and regional fragmentation on Beijing's actions.

Chinese Initiative and Escalation

Beijing's ability to enforce its maritime territorial claims has varied significantly since 1949. Fravel (2011) notes that, until 2010, China adopted a delaying strategy over its maritime claims, although one punctuated by periods of limited escalation (292). Throughout much of the Cold War, Chinese leaders asserted historical rights to islands in both seas, but they were generally content to foster joint exploration and utilization efforts rather than attempt to seize direct control. Indeed, due to limited naval capability, Beijing typically lagged behind the island occupation and reclamation efforts of other maritime claimants, including Vietnam, the Philippines, and Taiwan. However, from 1988, China raced to occupy some of the most politically and strategically desirable marine features in the Seas, sparking direct conflict with Vietnam in Johnson Reef (where 74 Vietnamese were killed), and concluding with Beijing's occupation of Mischief Reef in 1994. Afterwards, China once again adopted a delaying strategy, consolidating its gains and managing the diplomatic fallout from the successive clashes. During that period, Beijing signed codes of conduct with the Philippines and ASEAN and joined UNCLOS.

Since 2010, however, China has taken more assertive maritime positions, feeding these claims into broader narratives of geopolitical and sociocultural grievance. President Xi in particular has tied his political legitimacy to a "China Dream" of national rejuvenation, where "reclamation" of historic waters and territories feature prominently. Moreover, while aboard the guided missile destroyer *Haikou*, Xi directly linked China's economic success to a powerful military and greater assertiveness over sovereignty concerns. Thus, in addition to the security benefits of forward deployed surveillance and military assets on reclaimed land features, asserting maritime claims provides "the healing of a sort of psychological wound in the collective Chinese mind. Importantly, demonstrating the power to close the gap also accrues credibility for the current Chinese leadership and helps solidify the place of the Communist Party as the ruling entity of the Chinese state" (Dutton 2014, 3). The importance of nationalist appeals has only increased as the Chinese GDP growth rate has steadily slowed from a high of 14.23 percent in 2007 to a projected target of 6.1 percent in 2019.[8]

As these maritime claims gained political salience, China separately embarked on a comprehensive military modernization project. Its rapid qualitative and quantitative increase in coercive capabilities has been exhaustively documented, so this book will only touch on a few crucial points. The government claims its military budget expanded from RMB25.1 billion in 1989 to RMB720.2 billion in 2013, a twenty-eight-fold increase that is nevertheless smaller than thirty-five-fold increase in the country's GDP over that same period (GlobalSecurity.org). However, that number likely understates or hides parts of the military budget, according to many non-Chinese estimates of publicly available and classified data. The Stockholm International Peace Research Institute's estimates, for example, are typically 1.5 times larger than the official defense budget. Their 2013 estimate was RMB1.114 trillion (US$179.8 billion), and their latest 2018 estimate is RMB1.654 trillion (US$249.9 billion) (Stockholm International Peace Research Institute). Whatever the measure, China has had the second largest military budget since around 2006. These funds have fueled successive waves of military modernization, with the PLAN and the People's Liberation Army Air Force (PLAAF) most recently acquiring advanced systems from Russia and producing 4.5 and fifth generation fighters, nuclear submarines, and indigenously developed and built

---

8   2007 data from the World Bank: https://data.worldbank.org/indicator/NY.GDP. MKTP.KD.ZG?locations=CN; 2019 projection from CNBC: https://www.cnbc. com/2019/01/21/china-2018-gdp-china-reports-economic-growth-for-fourth-quarter-year.html.

aircraft carriers. The PLAN is the world's second largest navy by tonnage and has the most major combatant vessels (over 130). These include two aircraft carriers and "an overall battle force of approximately 350 ships and submarines" (Department of Defense 2020, 44). Similarly, the PLAAF is the world's second largest air force, with approximately 2,000 combat and around 400 transport and logistics aircraft (Department of Defense 2020, 166). According to the RAND Corporation, within 90 miles of its shore (i.e., a Taiwan scenario), China now possesses or can create an advantageous military balance against American forces in two of nine domains and parity within four domains (Heginbotham et al. 2017). Around 800 miles out (i.e., a Spratly Islands scenario relevant for this book's analysis), the US regains some advantages, but Beijing can still create military parity in four of nine domains.

Furthermore, improvements to China's maritime law enforcement services are as important to its gray zone strategy as those to its conventional naval forces. China consolidated four paramilitary maritime services into the CCG in 2013. These included the China Marine Surveillance, the China Maritime Police, the Fisheries Enforcement Service, and the General Administration of Customs. Prior to consolidation, these services were upgrading the number, tonnage, and capabilities of their vessels, allowing them to operate in blue water. The PLAN transferred several frigates to the CCG's predecessors, although most were stripped of their main guns. That said, several new acquisitions possess significant armaments, including 76mm cannons on the Type 718 and Type 818 cutters, high-capacity water cannons, interceptor boats, and on-board helicopter landing and maintenance equipment. In addition, the CCG has expanded the variety of crafts under its command, significantly diversifying the types of missions it can accomplish, including offshore surveillance, interdiction and search, and enforcement operations. CCG vessels have also been upgraded with new detection and surveillance systems, and China has consolidated and upgraded the supply, repair, and intelligence facilities supporting these forces, expanding the operational capability and range of even some coastal vessels. According to Erickson and Martinson (2019), as of 2020, the CCG alone can call upon 17,000 personnel manning 1,300 ships, 260 of which are capable of operating in blue water. The breakdown in ship types and growth in each category are listed in Table 2 below.

Table 2: China Coast Guard Forces (Erickson and Martinson, 2019, 110, Exhibit 7-1)[9]

Force Level (Type, Displacement in Tons)	2005	2010	2017	2020
Oceangoing Patrol Ships (2,500-10,000)	3	5	55	60
Regional Patrol Ships (1,000-2,499)	25	30	70	80
Regional Patrol Combatants (500-999)	30	65	100	120
Coastal Patrol Ships (100-499)	350	400	450	450
Inshore Patrol Boats/ Minor Craft (<100)	500+	500+	600+	600+
Total	900+	1,000+	1,275+	1,300+

Beyond the CCG, Beijing has several other maritime organizations of note, including the China Maritime Safety Administration and China Rescue and Salvage. The most important, however, is the PAFMM. Derek Grossman and Logan Ma describe the PAFMM as "a government-supported armed fishing force of unknown strength that resides under the direct command and control of the People's Liberation Army (PLA). It has existed for decades and augments CCG and PLAN operations in the region" (Grossman and Ma 2020). Each PAFMM group is locally supported by both civilian and military administrative systems that aggregate up from municipal- to province-level national defense mobilization committees. As with the PLA and People's Armed Police (PAP), the Central Military Commission ultimately oversees and directs these forces. While the majority of militia forces are civilians working in marine industries like fishing, some PAFMM garrisons have established elite, standing elements with specialized training in intelligence, surveillance, and reconnaissance (ISR) and more capable,

---

9   This table only includes ships under national-level command, excluding provincial, county, or municipal vessels. See also Erickson, Hickey, and Holst (2019, Table 1).

ocean-going vessels (Axe, 2019; Kennedy and Erickson, 2016). Although PAFMM vessels are typically unarmed, some carry water cannons and light weapons, and many have used their sheer bulk to ram, interfere with, or block other vessels' missions and tasks. For example, Erickson and Kennedy (2015) catalogue how a fishing trawler attempted to snag the USNS Impeccable's towed array cable in March 2009. During the Scarborough Shoal and HYSY 981 oilrig standoff, these crafts physically obstructed Philippine and Vietnamese forces, respectively, from entering core maritime territories. Numbers for the PAFMM are hard to come by, but at least eighty-four are purpose-built ships equipped with water cannons and reinforced steel hulls for ramming (Yeo 2019). Their numbers dwarf other regional states' military forces, and only Vietnam possesses a (smaller and less capable) force equivalent to this paramilitary service (see Phuong 2020). The dual civilian-military nature of the PAFMM and the fact that fishing boats can suddenly become ramming vessels complicates any military response. Regional militaries may only have lethal options available in protecting themselves against, say, bumping or ramming actions. And while any military ship could easily destroy one or multiple PAFMM trawlers, that would clearly escalate a conflict and potentially allow China to claim an attack against nominally "civilian" victims. Moreover, the sheer number and relative inexpensiveness of repairing or purchasing these ships means China can afford a high loss ratio, outlasting regional navies in contests of attrition.

Overall, China now possesses numerous naval, air, law enforcement, and "civilian" units capable of conducting a diverse range of coercive operations to extend its control over marine territory. However, for this book, the salient point is not the sheer growth in China's power, but how it chooses to use that power. Russian operations in Georgia, Crimea, and eastern Ukraine provide a clarifying contrast to China's actions in the South and East China Seas. At the point of dispute, attribution was far more ambiguous in the Russian cases. The use of cyber attacks and "little green men" allowed Moscow to deny its direct involvement, delaying a response until its forces could seize critical logistics points and achieve strategic goals against limited, local opposition. In essence, ambiguous attribution facilitated Russia's strategy of control through denial, where a *fait accompli* substantially reduced the risks to troops and costs of seizure.

By contrast, attribution has never been a problem in the Chinese maritime cases under consideration here. In each, Chinese ships and aircraft—both civilian and military—flew national flags. During the 2010 trawler collision, for example, state media confirmed that hundreds of Chinese commercial ships were near the Senkaku Islands, and the Japanese Coast Guard used a Chinese-language recording to demand that the Minjinyu 5179 (the Chinese vessel involved in the collision) leave. Similarly, during the 2014 oilrig standoff, Beijing released videos of Vietnamese ships ramming CCG ones, clearly acknowledging China's official presence in those waters. Indeed, national attribution is critical to Beijing's strategy. Russia sought direct, physical control of land, with ambiguous attribution serving to confuse, delay, and reduce responses (especially military ones) by third parties. China, by contrast, seeks political domination of "unoccupiable" territory. While Beijing cannot completely foreclose access to the Seas even with its large commercial, paramilitary, and military fleets, it can use them to force other vessels away and prevent interference with Chinese commercial and territorial operations. In short, China seeks compliance. Clear national attribution facilitates this by linking its large number of PAFMM boats to support by well-equipped and capable CCG and PLAN ships, if needed. Beijing follows a strategy of control by punishment where clear, not ambiguous, attribution lets other military and commercial vessels know whose rules to follow.

The observation flows from the cases. Barring only the Vietnam one, each began with at most a minor departure from the status quo. Beijing seizes upon these departures and surprises regional governments by flooding the zone with numerically superior CCG and PAFMM vessels, occasionally backed by the PLAN and PLAAF. During the Senkaku nationalization crisis, the Tokyo Governor was finalizing plans to purchase the islands from its private Japanese owner, amounting to a political victory for right-wing Japanese politicians. The Noda administration swept in and purchased the islands instead. They viewed this as a de-escalatory mechanism preventing further politicization of the ownership question. Indeed, the territories themselves were already under Japanese administrative control, following their handover from the US according to the 1971 Okinawa Reversion Treaty. Nevertheless, Japan spotted eighty-one vessels in the island's contiguous zone (12-24 nm) in September 2012, a significant increase from two the month before. Over one hundred vessels were sighted over the following two months, with several dozen coming within 12 nm of the islands (Japanese Ministry of Foreign Affairs, 2019).[10] (See Figure 1 below.) The

---

10   Graphic located at https://www.mofa.go.jp/files/000465486.pdf.

Japanese Coast Guard deployed half its fleet in response, but the operational challenge of monitoring and preventing multiple Chinese incursions and demonstrating Japanese presence rapidly degraded that force's readiness and response capabilities. Similarly, in March 2014, the Philippines government was conducting a routine resupply of the *Sierra Madre*, a former US tank landing ship that was deliberately run aground fifteen years earlier to serve as a marine outpost on the Second Thomas Shoal. Manila was surprised when two CCG ships blocked and drove off the Philippine vessels during this mission (Green et al. 2017, 184).

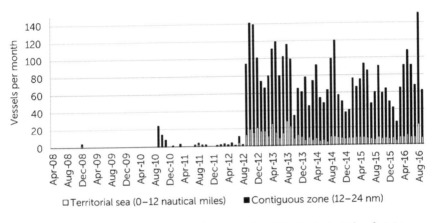

Figure 1: Number of Chinese Vessels Spotted within Senkaku Islands Waters

In flooding the conflict zone with ships, China can control the pace, intensity, and duration of disputes. Beijing's local escalation dominance allows it to overwhelm or outlast Asian opponents, with its conventional military superiority containing disputes at the sub-conventional level. Introducing ships to monitor and confront rival forces, demonstrate presence, and deny access (for short periods) to certain land features and even stretches of open water rapidly raises a respondent's costs of confrontation. In the Vietnam oilrig standoff, China initially sent four civilian vessels, including HYSY 981, on May 2, 2014, to conduct exploratory drilling within Vietnamese waters. The Vietnamese Coast Guard and Fisheries Resources Surveillance dispatched six ships in response. Within a day, China deployed forty vessels to escort HYSY 981, a mix of CCG, civilian fishing, and possibly PLAN ships. At its height, as many as 136 Chinese government ships (including both CCG and PLAN vessels) and "hundreds" of fishing boats surrounded HYSY 981. Moreland in Erickson and Martinson (2019) argues that Vietnam's retaliation—multiple vessels ramming and colliding with CCG and PAFMM ships over a two-month period—demonstrated Hanoi's resolve and produced a better outcome than in the Philippine cases. However, the picket prevented these forces from directly attacking or driving off HYSY 981, although this Vietnamese pressure may have prompted HYSY 981 to announce the "completion" its survey one month sooner than planned. Moreover, the sheer number of available Chinese vessels allows Beijing to prosecute multiple operations with sufficient forces simultaneously. In 2012, Beijing contested Japan's nationalization of the Senkakus only a couple weeks after driving Philippine ships out of the Scarborough Shoal. Similarly, as emphasized by Figure 1, dozens of Chinese crafts have continued patrolling waters near the Senkaku Islands since 2012, even as Beijing deployed additional vessels in disputes with the Philippines, Vietnam, and the US and in support of its land reclamation projects in the Spratly Islands group.

Even economically and militarily advanced regional states cannot match these paramilitary capabilities, and so must choose military escalation, using their own non-lethal forces (when available) against more numerous adversaries in a costly attrition strategy, or acquiescing to Chinese demands. Military escalation is itself risky, as China's conventional PLAN and PLAAF forces are also quantitatively and often qualitatively superior to those of other countries. Furthermore, Beijing's possession of strategic initiative produces a wider chilling effect. While China cannot simultaneously control or deny all the territory it claims against challengers, by selectively applying coercive pressure in specific instances and prevailing, it signals to other actors that they must accept Beijing's rules and restrictions to avoid similar punishment. After China seized control of the Scarborough Reef in 2012, for example, Manila avoided further contestation and escalation, even as CCG ships turned away Philippine commercial vessels from long-standing fishing areas. Although the US, the Republic of Korea, and Japanese militaries contest China's Air Defense Identification Zone (ADIZ), civilian airlines comply with these regulations. So long as China possesses escalation dominance, regional actors begin any dispute at a serious disadvantage in available forces and initiative, inviting further caution and cementing adherence to Chinese preferences on maritime governance. And unlike Russia, Beijing benefits from clear attribution: flying the Chinese flag demonstrates presence and monitoring of compliance.

As seen in the Appendix, the respondent's military power has little influence in these conflicts. Note that regional states' navies outclass and can easily defeat CCG and PAFMM forces. But using military power against nominally civilian forces could invite reprisals from the PLAN and PLAAF, neutralizing this option. The issue is political, whether a target is willing to accept escalation costs and Chinese military retaliation in exchange for the contested territory's strategic and economic value. Importantly, this implicates American alliance commitments to Japan and the Philippines, as well as its broader interest in regional peace, as only Washington can break China's local escalation dominance. Even as Chinese assertiveness has pushed regional countries to seek closer security cooperation with Washington, the US has generally avoided deeper entanglement in these issues, only gradually providing clearer military commitments to regional partners. The following section examines how this reluctance has facilitated China's strategy, and how geostrategic shifts increasingly undermine the American approach.

Pivotal Deterrence: The US Security Strategy

Washington has traditionally pursued a policy of "pivotal deterrence" toward Asian security conflicts. It opposes changes to the status quo by military force, no matter which state initiates. US alliances deter adversaries like Russia, China, and North Korea. But they may simultaneously prompt allies themselves to escalate disputes under American protection or entrap Washington in unwanted conflicts. To offset these risks, the US frequently engages in "strategic ambiguity," leaving undefined exactly how far it will support its partner in order to encourage restraint. In the 1974, for example, the US worked closely with South Vietnam to fight the Vietnam War. However, Washington denied Saigon's request for direct naval support in the Battle of the Paracel Islands against China, seeking to de-escalate hostilities. State Department Spokesman John King stated, "We have no claims ourselves and we are not involved in the dispute. It is for the claimants to solve among themselves" (Associated Press 1974; Reuters 1974). With its preponderance of power, Washington can swing conflicts towards its ally or adversary, thereby containing conflict from all sides.

This "pivotal deterrence" approach stands in marked contrast to the more commonly known "extended deterrence." The latter, as Paul Huth (1988) describes, is "a confrontation in which the policymakers of one state ('defender') threaten the use of force against another state ('potential attacker') in an attempt to prevent the state from using military force against an ally—or territory controlled by the ally ('protégé') of the defender." It is foundationally a form of interstate signaling, with one country threatening another with coercive power on behalf of a third state if certain conditions are violated. To be effective, such threats must be unambiguous, often public, so as to engage a state's reputation and costly signaling mechanisms, and usually made during the early stages of a conflict. Extended deterrence represents significant interest alignment between the defender and protégé. As Cesa (2010) describes, "extended" allies possess the same primary and secondary interests in an alliance and preference ordering. The defender has decided that greater entrapment risk is an acceptable exchange for improved deterrence against the adversary.

But in other cases, these secondary interests diverge sharply, and any conflict over them—whether initiated by the adversary *or* the ally—could harm or derail coordination on the primary interest. In this case, defenders may prefer a pivotal deterrence approach, selectively promising, withholding, or making ambiguous its commitment and conditions. *Both* the adversary and ally should then avoid adventurism for fear of tilting the pivot towards their enemy. This strategy reduces entrapment risk and focuses partners on the primary, shared interest animating an alliance. Crawford (2003) notes that pivots are especially effective when:

1. The pivot is status quo-oriented, while both the adversary and the ally are revisionists. If the ally is also status quo-oriented, the pivot would simply side with it in an extended deterrence strategy.

2. The pivot has a preponderance of power over both states, and its contribution to either actor would decisively shift the balance in that country's favor.

If it has preponderant power, the pivot can more effectively execute its strategy when the policy issue being contested is of vital importance to the adversaries, but of secondary importance to itself. In that case, pivots can more credibly threaten to tilt away from either actor.

The US has followed a pivotal deterrence strategy with regard to Asian maritime territorial disputes. Washington possesses preponderant military power compared to any East or Southeast Asian country. China's build-up and modernization of its armed forces since the 1990s is eroding this advantage, but the US can still create favorable balances in several combat and operational domains (Heginbotham et al. 2017). Further, these territorial disputes are a American secondary interest. Washington is primarily concerned with freedom of navigation, as well as preventing or defusing conflicts that would jeopardize open access and transit and regional development. In accordance, although at least six Asian countries make overlapping sovereignty claims, the US avoided extending alliance protection to marine features until 2010 so as not to bolster any one country's claim. Even then, it "takes no position on competing sovereignty claims to land features in the region" (US Department of Defense 2015, 5–6). Instead, successive administrations have pushed for a negotiated resolution to these issues among disputants and have "oppose[d] any attempt to use coercion or force to settle disputes."[11]

We can see this strategy at work in the cases examined here. Particularly in the earlier ones, the US attempted to dissuade both China and its partner from further conflict. During the 2010 trawler collision, Obama administration officials privately criticized Japan's decision to arrest the ship's captain and "treat the incident as a dangerous provocation," when it could have been de-escalated quietly (Green et al. 2017, 74). Washington called the dispute a "narrow issue" that should be resolved bilaterally and peacefully between China and Japan (US Department of State, 2010). Later commenting on a September 23, 2010 meeting between American and Japanese officials, US NSC Senior Director for Asian Affairs Jeffrey Bader stated that the administration was ambivalent about upholding the Mutual Defense Treaty over a sovereignty issue in which it had no position. It was "absurd" to think the US should be drawn into an armed conflict (Bader 2013, 107).

During the Scarborough Shoal standoff two years later, the Obama administration was similarly vague about whether the US-Philippine treaty covered any of Manila's maritime claims and refused direct military intervention against China. Washington ultimately attempted to orchestrate a mutual withdrawal of Chinese and Philippine forces from the Shoal, firmly directing Manila to "step back" after supposedly receiving a Chinese commitment to de-escalate (Green et al. 2017, 118; see also Erickson and Martinson 2019, 285).

Separately in that year, Japanese Prime Minister Noda thought he had received China's blessing for the central government to acquire the Senka-

---

11   https://www.state.gov/u-s-position-on-maritime-claims-in-the-south-china-sea/.

kus, as this would be less provocative than Tokyo Governor Ishihara's nationalization plan and "defang" this right-wing talking point. The Prime Minister announced his plan on July 7 without consulting Washington. At a bilateral meeting a day later, the American team doubted that Japan had in fact secured Chinese agreement and expressed concern that the US would be dragged into a conflict by an alliance partner. Beijing denounced Noda's plan, eventually deploying China Marine Surveillance, PAFMM, and PLAN vessels in dozens of incursions over the following months (Liff 2019, 212). Despite this escalation, many White House officials remained opposed to Japan's nationalization plan due to entrapment concerns (Green et al. 2017, 147). It was only three months later in September 2012 that US Secretary of Defense Leon Panetta confirmed to both Japan and China that the Mutual Defense Treaty (MDT) covered the Senkakus. An additional two months passed before the US declared it would not accept changes to Japan's *de facto* control of the islands (Oshima and Minemura 2012; see also Green et al. 2017, 141, 144).

In all three cases, the US triangulated between China and its local ally to de-escalate tensions. Washington refrained from affirming defense commitments until its partners coordinated on policy, and it pointedly refused to support their sovereignty claims to any of the territorial features. Measured according to ally restraint, pivotal deterrence was a success, as regional states de-escalated tensions and made conciliatory gestures towards China to retain US support.

However, this strategy is only truly effective when ambiguity simultaneously restrains adversaries. Here, the case evidence suggests that vague US policy—particularly whether alliances cover disputed territory—encouraged greater Chinese escalation. Beijing steadily increased coercive pressure until Washington directly confirmed that its defense pacts applied to these conflicts. In the Scarborough Shoal, CCG ships more aggressively challenged Philippine vessels, and Beijing threatened to deploy the PLAN to resolve the dispute (Green et al. 2017, 109). During the 2010 trawler collision incident, the US called for a bilateral resolution that preserved its neutrality in the underlying territorial disagreement and initially refused to support *de facto* Japanese administration of the Senkakus. During this same period, Beijing conducted increasing numbers of maritime law enforcement patrols, normalizing its presence missions there. It also steadily escalated diplomatic and commercial pressure on Tokyo, suspending negotiations over oil and natural gas exploration in the East China Sea, parliamentarian visits, discussions on coal and air rights, sister city programs, and even musical events. Moreover, China is even less restrained against countries without a US security commitment. Beijing only threatened PLAN involvement against the Philippines in 2012, for example. But against Vietnam, PLAN and PLAAF units arrived with days, even introducing amphibious transports and fixed-wing attack aircraft to the theater.

Once the US affirms alliance commitments, however, Chinese maritime activities either decreased (Japan) or leveled off (the Philippines). With Japan, Washington affirmed that the MDT covered disputed territories on September 23, 2010, September 17–18, 2012, and April 24, 2014. The five weeks following each declaration saw a 42%, 67%, and 49% decrease, respectively, in Chinese incursions into Japan's contiguous maritime zones.[12] Even tepid application of US defense commitments may have induced Chinese caution, contrary to the pivotal deterrence expectations. Twelve days after the Philippine Navy began arresting Chinese fishermen during the Scarborough Shoal standoff, US Marine Corps Lieutenant General Duane Thiessen vaguely affirmed that the MDT committed the US to supporting Manila. He stated that the treaty "guarantees that we get involved in each other's defense and that is self-explanatory" (Agence France-Presse 2012). American officials did not confirm this off-the-cuff remark to a Philippine reporter. Nevertheless, Beijing did withdraw two maritime administration ships, evidently as a good faith demonstration of its desire to defuse the situation. President Obama officially confirmed this alliance understanding on June 15, shortly before it brokered a Sino-Philippine agreement for mutual withdrawal. Finally, although Vietnam does not enjoy a US defense commitment, Hanoi called for US engagement and support to confront China over the HYSY 981 standoff. Washington pledged $18 million to support the Vietnam Coast Guard on May 18, 2014, while Japan announced that it would more quickly provide maritime patrol vessels to Hanoi four days later. China then redeployed HYSY 981 further away from Vietnam, reduced the size of its declared exclusion zone, and ultimately withdrew a month earlier than scheduled.

Overall, while ambiguity may have deterred Chinese escalation in the past, Beijing currently responds to clarity about US commitments. Crawford's

---

12   Data drawn from Japan Coast Guard (https://www.kaiho.mlit.go.jp/mission/sen kaku/senkaku.html) and Green et al. (2017, 75).

theory can explain why the pivotal deterrence strategy has been unable to induce adversary restraint. Beijing's expanded naval capabilities are dislodging the US as a pivot, allowing China to achieve its objectives despite American and allied resistance. Although the US is globally far more powerful, Beijing can create a local balance of forces that in certain scenarios achieves parity with American and allied militaries across a range of combat domains, particularly in air superiority and naval access and survivability (Fuell 2014; Heginbotham et al. 2017; Lague and Lim 2019). China's paramilitary forces are as important, if not more important, than these increasing conventional capabilities. The US and regional states are unable to meet CCG and PAFMM challenges symmetrically using their own paramilitary units. Washington does conduct FONOPs to signal its concern for freedom of navigation (Panda 2018). But these operations do not degrade the CCG and PAFMM's ability to erode or threaten regional states' control of land features, preserving local Chinese escalation dominance. (Cooper and Poling 2019; Lan 2018; Roy 2018; Valencia 2017). Moreover, as Asian maritime security is a secondary US interest, Beijing can widen differences in interest intensity through selective confrontation. For example, China actively contests non-militarized territorial claims by regional states, but is more circumspect in challenging US Navy FONOPs.

Overall, the eroding American pivot unbalances the triad. US ambiguity restrains its security partners, but emboldens the adversary. As a consolidated actor, China can take advantage of US-partner divisions to effect further changes to the status quo. As the power balance shifts from preponderance to peer competition, a pivot's ambiguity emboldens the stronger adversary, particularly if the former cannot rapidly intervene in a conflict before that adversary achieves a *fait accompli.*

These dynamics have gradually pushed the US into making firmer regional commitments. Indeed, Washington openly welcomed closer alliance coordination by late 2013. During the East China Sea ADIZ controversy that year, South Korea significantly enlarged its own zone in a direct challenge to China's actions. The US supported this move, praising Seoul for "pursuing this action in a responsible, deliberate fashion by prior consultations with not just the United States, but also, very importantly, with Japan and China" and helping to "avoid [...] confusion because of the cooperation and coordination in advance" (Psaki 2013). Similarly, due to the closer coordination generated by Beijing's previous incursions, Tokyo and Washington much more quickly crafted a coordinated response, conducting joint flythroughs within days of China's ADIZ announcement. Moreover, Chinese assertiveness is fostering greater regional consolidation even beyond consultation with Washington. Regional accession to UNCLOS, the Philippines' willingness to submit its Scarborough Shoal claims to international arbitration, and ASEAN and international support for Vietnam's status quo-oriented stand against China over the HYSY 981 oilrig suggest that other Asian states may more fully support the status quo, or at least resist Beijing's attempts to change it.

Consequently, in eroding the US pivotal position, China is also decreasing Washington's need to triangulate between it and its neighbors. It is important, however, to emphasize the contingency of this implication. All South China Sea claimants have established outposts or reclaimed land on disputed islands, possibly in contravention of UNCLOS. Vietnam, for example, has dredged over 110 acres, while Malaysia has built installations on five Spratly Island features. Beijing's efforts dwarf these projects, and other states are increasingly unable to maintain or supply their outposts against Chinese interference. But if China suddenly ceased these activities, rival claimants may resume their own reclamation efforts, especially to blunt Chinese gains made over the past decade. Further, Tokyo and Manila at least would do so with assurances that their administration of contested territory falls under American alliances. The US remains reluctant to side with any state's sovereignty claims, emphasizing instead its support for UNCLOS's maritime definitions and interpretations against expansive Chinese assertions of "historical rights" (Cooper and Glaser 2020). But, the gaps, brittleness, and contesting interpretations of this maritime settlement spur Asian sovereignty disputes and complicate any future US strategy, as the following section details.

The Maritime Settlement: Regional Fragmentation and Weak Legitimacy

Northeast and Southeast Asia suffer from an "institutional vacuum" (Calder and Ye 2004; Pempel 2010; Rozman 2011). Despite robust economic growth and regional integration, significant security disputes and overlapping territorial claims threaten the peace and development those countries have achieved. Few formal and effective interstate organizations exist to manage these challenges, to limit or deter conflict, or to generate political momentum towards a comprehensive territorial and maritime settlement. States proclaim their respect for the status quo and adherence to UNCLOS, but each advances their own interpretation of the convention that aligns with their strategic preferences. In short, the region lacks a clear consensus on standards of conduct. The situation, as Pempel (2010) notes, "reflect[s] the underlying wariness of their members about one another as well as their collective reluctance to surrender substantial national sovereignty to such regional bodies. East Asian governments have approached the new regionalism as tentatively as the cautious man in the Korean admonition that 'one should tap even a stone bridge before crossing'" (230). Further, what institutions they do have, like ASEAN, operate on consensus decision-making rules. While this preserves the veneer of regional comity, each actor effectively possesses a veto on the organization's policies. China has exploited this political fragmentation and brittle consensus to neutralize collective political, military, and legal responses to its maritime operations and to advance its own legal standards for territorial sovereignty and naval conduct. Without counterbalancing US initiatives and commitment, regional states lack the cohesion, guarantees, and political incentives to reach a comprehensive maritime settlement based on UNCLOS and relevant international law.

Washington's position on UNCLOS and the Asian maritime settlement spurs this fragmentation. Despite the central role it played in drafting and establishing the convention in 1974, the US has never ratified it, even after exceptions were carved out in 1994 to accommodate American demands on exploring and exploiting seabed and Arctic resources (Bromund, Carafano, and Schaefer, 2018; Locklear 2012; United Nations 1994). Since Ronald Reagan, Washington has viewed most of UNCLOS as customary law and acted according to its rules. But this failed to prevent charges of hypocrisy from China, and, more importantly, Asian states have questioned whether the US will follow arbitration provisions that it has rejected in other legal contexts (Bower and Poling 2012; Reagan 1983).[13] As I find in separate research, *de facto* adherence to international treaties inevitably leads to concerns among members about how committed the "informal" partner is. Its refusal to accede raises doubts about whether it adheres only to "low cost" provisions or will agree to the "high cost" ones as well. Formal members

---

13 The US Navy is a particularly strong advocate for accession and already follows UNCLOS guidelines. See https://www.jag.navy.mil/organization/code_10_law_of_the_sea.htm; Cardin (2016); Denyer (2016); Moore (2004); Slavin (2016); Sullivan (2016); Wyne (2016).

also worry that this country may seek a better deal with third parties. This undercuts American appeals for regional states to settle maritime disputes peacefully. Washington cannot use UNCLOS mechanisms to shape this process. Asian countries are uncertain if Washington will accept and respect any agreements they make, particularly if these require US military backing, economic inducements, or political support.

In addition, Beijing has pushed for a "new type of Great Power relations," where the US respects China's "core interests" in return for more cooperative policies (Zeng and Breslin 2016). Such a condominium, however, would allow Beijing greater autonomy and authority over the East and South China Seas, exacerbating fears that the US seeks regional agreement to improve relations with China, not foster a lasting and coherent settlement (Li and Xu 2014). Foundationally, the US posture toward a maritime resolution is reactive, much like its pivotal deterrence approach to alliances. Washington has conducted little security institution-building in Southeast and Northeast Asia, contributing to the regions' organizational vacuums. While desiring a peaceful settlement to sovereignty issues, it generally expects regional states to develop a comprehensive solution on their own. However, Washington provides few public indications of what terms it will accept and what support it will provide, doing little to help regional states overcome disagreements. The US recognizes and supports the continuation of allies' *de facto* control over certain maritime land features pending such a settlement, extending security guarantees to Japan and the Philippines as discussed above. But these decisions stem from narrowly defined alliance commitments that do not address the political, economic, and diplomatic challenges that a lasting agreement must solve. Without that focal leadership, local states have fewer incentives or ability to create an effective settlement.

As a result, and because of ASEAN's consensus decision-making process and regional pre-eminence, belligerents need only peel off one or two countries to block collective responses. The *Philippines v. China* arbitration case is illustrative.[14] Vietnam strongly supported Manila's legal position, while Taiwan joined China in challenging the tribunal's jurisdiction to hear the

---

14 The Philippines' Notification and Statement of Claim is available at https://www. dfa.gov.ph/images/UNCLOS/Notification%20and%20Statement%20of%20 Claim%20on%20West%20Philippine%20Sea.pdf. The Permanent Court of Arbitration's decision is available at https://pca-cpa.org/wp-content/uploads/sites/ 6/2016/07/PH-CN-20160712-Award.pdf.

case. Indonesia and Malaysia—whose territorial claims against China were strengthened by the ruling—generally did not comment on the proceedings, instead urging self-restraint by all claimants (Kyodo News 2016).[15] Without regional support for the Philippines' position, China only needed to persuade Manila to change course. During an October 2016 state visit to Beijing, newly elected Philippine President Rodrigo Duterte secured $24 billion from China for his infrastructure development plan and billions more in business contracts and public financing agreements, although little of that money has materialized (Lema and Perry 2018). Duterte also announced an economic and military "separation" from the US (although he almost immediately softened that declaration). Two months later, he agreed to "set aside" the tribunal's ruling in deference to China's position (Associated Press 2016; Hunt, Rivers, and Shoichet 2016). Moreover, Beijing traditionally prefers to settle disputes bilaterally, leveraging its greater power to extract better agreements from rivals (Rozman 2011, 309, 311). In line with this, China and the Philippines established a bilateral consultation mechanism at the Vice Ministerial-level preventing further "internationalization" of territorial disputes and bypassing ASEAN (Wong 2019). This mechanism is already under strain due to Beijing's and Manila's fundamental geostrategic and political differences (Mourdoukoutas 2019a, 2019b). But no alternative nor multilateral initiatives have replaced this framework.

Similarly, Vietnam garnered significant international support during the 2014 oilrig standoff. ASEAN (2014) issued a joint foreign ministers statement expressing "serious concerns over the ongoing developments in the South China Sea." The Philippines and Indonesia separately declared strong support for Hanoi's position, joining prior statements and offers of material assistance by Japan, the EU, the UK, and Australia. Despite this success, China broke up further ASEAN consolidation by pressuring Cambodia, then the body's chair, to keep territorial disputes off the ASEAN Summit's agenda (Agence France-Presse 2016; Reuters 2017).[16] Instead, ASEAN and Chi-

---

15   To be fair, as part of a previous filing, Indonesia claimed that "the so called 'nine-dotted-lines map' [...] clearly lacks international legal basis and is tantamount to upset the UNCLOS 1982." https://www.un.org/Depts/los/clcs_new/submissions_files/mysvnm33_09/idn_2010re_mys_vnm_e.pdf. However, Indonesian ministers provided contradictory statements on the arbitration, claiming that Indonesia was not a claimant, but might itself refer certain fishery disputes to the tribunal. See Parameswaran (2016).

16   For a comparative analysis for Cambodia's role in China's approach to ASEAN, see Kreuzer (2016).

na formally began discussions on a Code of Conduct (COC) for the South China Sea. But at the outset, Beijing rejected a binding agreement, and it has thus far secured supportive or neutral positions from Cambodia, Thailand, Malaysia, Indonesia, and Singapore (Thayer 2013). The COC is therefore less likely to contain robust (and still non-binding) restrictions on China's maritime operations (Quang 2019). Overall, the lack of regional diplomatic cohesion and the absence of a focal settlement around which Asian states can coalesce have allowed Beijing to undercut momentum towards a consolidated position against its maritime assertions (Denyer 2016).

China is attempting to fill the organizational vacuum with its own rules and standards and consolidate acceptance of its maritime operations and control. In line with past rising powers, Beijing cares about its international reputation and frames its maritime operations as aligned with international law (Gilady 2018; Goddard 2018). However, its particular interpretation of maritime rules attempts to shift legal standards to align with its strategic preferences through a process of norm contestation. Although it purports to follow UNCLOS, Beijing contends that the convention fails to account for maritime rights emerging from historic precedent and control. In particular, it claims the Nine-Dash Line found on Republic of China maps dating back to 1935 demonstrate Chinese authority over much of the South China Sea. It is therefore entitled to sovereign control within this area based on "historic rights," presenting a veneer of legality to their approach.[17] Further, China claims that other states will benefit from using this historic rights standard. It has never specified the exact coordinates of the Nine-Dash Line, whether historic rights use the same territorial definitions and grant the same exploitation rights as under UNCLOS, or what actions other nations or transiting vessels can and cannot do under this legal theory (Jennings 2019). But this ambiguity, Beijing argues, advances the prospects for a regional security settlement. Major General Yao Yunzhu, a senior fellow at the People's Liberation Army's Academy of Military Science, claims that under this approach, "China and other claimants [...] have more room to maneuver and to have more room to compromise" (Wong 2016).[18] The Permanent Court of Arbitration rejected this concept

---

17 For a Chinese view on historic rights, see Zheng (2015). For a response, see Dutton (2015). See also Webster (2015).

18 At the same time, the "historic rights" approach risks other states asserting similar authority over their own claims and against China's. See Halliden (2014).

as a basis for sovereign jurisdiction in 2016, but China continues to use the Line in its claims.[19] Indeed, Beijing views itself as a status quo actor in the region, noting that it has acted with "great restraint" as other states reclaimed land and built installations in prior decades (Chubb 2015; Mehta 2015). Without counterbalancing legal and political support for the Tribunal's interpretation of UNCLOS, particularly from the US, China can continue advancing alternative legal frameworks aligned with its territorial assertions.

Conclusion

Effective deterrence of gray zone challenges requires robust alliance institutions, coordination strategies, and policies. But the rapid increase in Chinese capabilities and Washington's ambiguous commitment to UNCLOS increasingly undermine the United States' ability to accomplish these tasks. Fortunately, the evidence presented in this chapter suggests that China can be deterred. When Washington tightens alliances and extends its defensive guarantees to disputed territory, Beijing halts escalation. However, political support for the maritime settlement will remain fragmented until and unless the US produces a cohesive set of rules governing territorial disputes and backs them with diplomatic, legal, and military support. The following chapter builds on the observations made here to provide three alternative strategies Washington can adopt to more effectively challenge Chinese incursions, produce a regionally accepted maritime settlement, and achieve its foreign and security policy objectives in the South and East China Seas.

---

19 The Arbitral Tribunal specifically rejected China's "historic rights" as a basis for sovereign jurisdiction in the Permanent Court of Arbitration Award, Section V(F)(d) (278), 117, http://www.pcacases.com/pcadocs/PH-CN%20-%2020160712%20-%20Award.pdf. See also Lee (2016).

CHAPTER 3

CONFRONTING CHINA'S GRAY ZONE STRATEGY

Introduction

Gray zone strategies are contests of initiative. Formal and extensive security coordination between allies serves as the critical, actionable variable for states to deter revisionist challenges. China's recent coercive paramilitary operations in the South and East China Seas follow this pattern, but Chapter Two details how two strategic shifts—increased Chinese capabilities and greater status quo orientation among regional states—are undercutting the foundations of the United States' pivotal deterrence strategy. While Washington has increased its coordination with regional partners, China can continue to probe the seams of American alliance commitments unless and until the US either develops comprehensive mechanisms to coordinate multilateral responses or accommodates China, exchanging greater recognition of Beijing's maritime interests for Chinese deference to more narrowly defined American goals.

The 2015 NDAA Asia-Pacific Maritime Security Strategy articulates three US security objectives for Asia's maritime zones:

1. Safeguard the freedom of the seas;
2. Deter conflict and coercion; and
3. Promote adherence to international law and standards.

This chapter offers three separate strategies aligning American resources with these objectives in the South and East China Seas. Each represents a different balance between these NDAA goals. First, the US can construct a grand bargain with Beijing through an *accommodation* strategy. Rather than raising its capabilities to accomplish more expansive goals or making policy concessions to partners/allies, Washington can instead recognize some of China's territorial sovereignty claims. In exchange, Beijing would accept American naval dominance and guarantees freedom of navigation. This would reduce the US security burden, allowing it to focus resources elsewhere. While regional states will undoubtedly object, even collectively they cannot prevent China and the US from reaching an agreement, nor are they likely to be able to undermine it once in place. However, this approach is risky. It assumes that China will become a satisfied, status quo state once Washington accommodates its maritime interests. If that assumption is wrong, the US will have a significantly harder time regaining access and corralling regional support for future initiatives. In total, the accommodation strategy achieves NDAA #2 by mollifying Chinese grievances. It accomplishes NDAA #1 and NDAA #3 by redefining maritime rules to more closely mirror Beijing's preferences, while securing Chinese acceptance of freedom of navigation.

Second, the US can salvage a *pivotal deterrence* strategy by reestablishing a preponderance of regional naval power. This strategy is the one most aligned with the US order of prioritization among the NDAA goals: protecting freedom of navigation while simultaneously avoiding entrapment on sovereignty questions. Washington would need to unilaterally enhance its coercive capabilities to once again possess a decisive edge over Chinese military *and* paramilitary forces. A renewed pivotal position would bolster US ability to secure freedom of the seas (NDAA #1) and deter coercion (NDAA #2), although this escalation dominance might increase the risk of US-China conflict. The strategy would also maintain the ambiguous American position towards maritime law and some alliance commitments. While US accession to UNCLOS advances the other two courses of action, it is unnecessary and perhaps even harmful to a pivotal deterrence approach. Indeed, the US should explicitly avoid certain types of military and political coordination with allies so as not to encourage renewed territorial revisionism by these states.

Finally, Washington can more firmly align with its Asian partners, completing the shift from pivotal to *extended deterrence*. Given recent Chinese assertiveness, regional states are already seeking closer ties with the US. But this strategy is the most politically difficult, requiring that Washington create a comprehensive maritime territorial settlement among allied countries and actively join, maintain, and participate in buttressing institutions. To be maximally effective, the US should also make the investments in coercive capabilities found in the second, pivotal deterrence option, demonstrating that it can support its allies at all points on the escalation ladder. But in return, the US should seize the strategic initiative and lock in a durable maritime settlement. The process of transitioning from pivotal to extended deterrence must be handled delicately so as to maximize US gains from this shift and ensure equitable burden sharing into the future. This strategy clearly accomplishes NDAA #1 and #3 but raises the risk of conflict with Beijing (NDAA #2).

This chapter delineates the objectives, frameworks, benefits, and costs of each strategic option below and concludes with some general observations about China's gray zone challenge. Which strategy the US should pick is a political choice beyond this book's scope. But the three differ on a foundational question: *from where does Washington think the largest threat to US interests emanates?* If direct political and possibly military conflict with China represents the worst outcome, then an accommodation strategy best reduces that risk and enhances the ability of both capitals to cooperate on wider issues of mutual interest. If, however, instability and conflict from any source most threatens the United States' maritime position, then a pivotal deterrence strategy will allow Washington to leverage renewed capabilities to de-escalate disputes at moderate cost. Finally, if Chinese domination of the Seas is unacceptable, then the US should switch firmly to an extended deterrence strategy.

While each option stems from unique assumptions, they also share the view that, absent power preponderance, ambiguity no longer advances US foreign policy objectives. In addition, the support or acquiescence of regional states is essential for any strategy's durability. As discussed in Chapter Two, China's gray zone strategy has exploited and accelerated fragmentation of the maritime status quo. Political cohesion, whether through attraction or coercion, is therefore necessary to prevent future revisionist challenges. Moreover, cost increases across these alternatives, but risk decreases. With an accommodation strategy, the US does not need to invest in capabilities to match the CCG and PAFMM. Indeed, Washington would effectively outsource certain components of the security regime to Chinese authority. Such agreement would only hold, however, if Beijing had stable, time-consistent preferences. If, instead of satisfying Chinese ambitions, American withdrawal emboldened them, the US would find itself in a significantly worse position from which to regain regional access. By contrast, an extended deterrence strategy requires significant investment in military and paramilitary capabilities to reestablish escalation dominance and local military preponderance and also substantial political capital in negotiating a comprehensive and durable territorial settlement. That said, with sufficient regional support, this approach might entice even Beijing's adherence, would hedge against renewed Chinese revisionism, and consolidate the political fragmentation that the CCP currently exploits to prosecute its gray zone strategy.

Accommodation

Key Elements:

- China clearly defines scope of territorial claims.
- US establishes understanding of and redlines for freedom of navigation and responses to violations.
- China and US exchange recognition and acceptance of these policies.

Freedom of navigation (NDAA #1) constitutes the primary American maritime interest in Asia, and the US Navy has conducted approximately thirty-two FONOPs since October 2015 in the South China Sea to challenge Chinese territorial claims and reinforce UNCLOS provisions.[20] These missions risk conflict with PLAN and CCG forces, and they have not halted gray zone coercion of regional states. However, the US can decrease its security costs and prevent escalation through direct negotiation and cooperation with China, achieving the NDAA goals in part by redefining their scope and meaning. Under this accommodation strategy, Washington would trade recognition of Chinese territorial claims and sphere of influence in exchange for general guarantees of freedom of navigation and agreement on US redlines. The two countries must reach a clear understanding on what constitutes freedom of the seas, the extent of China's maritime claims, and a set of rules establishing the boundary between these two policies. But if successful, the US would achieve its foundational maritime objectives, while satisfying China's territorial demands. In essence, this strategy removes the locus of maritime conflict between the two countries, potentially converting China into a status quo state.

Accommodation rests on three pillars. First, China must clearly define the boundaries of its maritime claims, including their territorial seas, contiguous zones, and exclusive economic zones. It must also specify what rules it expects transiting states to follow within those areas. Does Beijing abide by UNCLOS there, and how does it interpret the Convention's provisions?

---

20 The US Navy also conducted approximately forty transits through the Taiwan Strait during that time.

Or does China's leadership have different expectations of passage and conduct under "historic rights?" Simply obtaining such a statement will require significant and careful American effort. China has purposely avoided clearly demarcating the Nine-Dash Line, increasing its bargaining leverage and space. Once the US expresses interest in accommodation, Beijing faces further incentives to withhold these demarcations until it has extracted maximal concessions just for coming to the table. Washington could bolster its negotiating leverage by increasing military spending and readiness to respond to Chinese maritime provocations. It can then trade concessions in the American force posture for clear declarations by Beijing. Alternatively, the US can impose deadlines for Chinese responses, threatening to switch to an extended deterrence strategy unless Beijing meets certain markers. (However, this hedge carries important, self-contradictory drawbacks discussed below.) In either case, Washington should aim to "lock down" the definitions, exceptions, and limits of Chinese territorial claims and maritime rules in the East and South China Seas, leaving little room for future disagreements about interpretation and scope.

Of course, Beijing will demand symmetrical clarity from the US. As the second pillar in this strategy, Washington must establish its definition of and redlines for freedom of navigation. What activities fall under legitimate commercial and military purposes for all states, and what rights do sovereigns have within their territorial seas, contiguous zones, and exclusive economic zones? How should international law define those three areas, particularly when it comes to past and future island-building/land reclamation by China and other regional states? What redlines does the US possess, and what responses will violations engender? Clearly answering this last question is critical to the condominium's durability. America must demonstrate its willingness to enforce the agreement—using military force if necessary—for China to forgo future territorial and maritime claims based on its new, more advantageous position. US accession to UNCLOS—not simply informal adherence—would be particularly helpful in solidifying this strategic pillar. *Ad hoc* concessions will do little to reassure China of American intentions. Indeed, Beijing can point to the United States' continued refusal to accede to UNCLOS despite the 1994 exceptions as an indication of Washington's lack of credibility on maritime settlements. Formally joining the Convention will demonstrate commitment and tie US policy to internationally recognized rules defining marine features.

Regional states will object to this "new type of great power relations." Their current willingness to pursue remedies through UNCLOS and legal tribunals suggests that they believe global institutions will eventually adjudicate the matter "fairly" according to mutually agreed rules. US-Chinese condominium bypasses these institutions. This weakens regional states' incentives to continue observing broader Convention guidelines on, say, resource conservation and usage, potentially harming other US interests. As a third pillar in the accommodation strategy, Washington must mollify these concerns to prevent legal and even military reprisals to this new agreement by Japan, the Philippines, Vietnam, and Taiwan, among others. These countries are unlikely to be convinced that satisfying China's territorial demands will convert Beijing into a status quo power. And they will be particularly concerned that China is misusing its now stronger position to violate the bargain and further extend maritime control. Washington and Beijing can address some of these concerns by more fully backing UNCLOS,[21] or establishing specialized institutions addressing Asian territorial or transit disputes and offering smaller states voice and voting powers. In addition, the US could extend greater military assistance and arms transfers to these states, further hedging against Chinese abrogation of the settlement. Finally, Washington could lean on its security and economic ties to Japan, the Philippines, and Taiwan to gain their acceptance of this policy.

To be fair, these measures are unlikely to work. Even with new transfers of conventional US equipment, regional states will remain largely unable to contest Chinese military and paramilitary strength. Nor can they rely upon American support or neutrality towards their territorial claims once Washington has embarked on accommodation. Regional acceptance of a US-China agreement will therefore be brittle. Countries will attempt to bypass this new regime to advance their own sovereignty claims, effectively becoming revisionist actors. If the US does provide new arms, recipients may be tempted to use these capabilities against each other rather than turning on Beijing, with American administrations less able to compel restraint. At the limit, states may seek advanced capabilities outside of the US arsenal, such as intermediate range ballistic missiles or even nuclear weapons. Unlike for Washington, maritime sovereignty issues are central concerns for these countries, raising the risk that local nations will use

---

21   However, having bypassed UNCLOS guidelines to create the US-China agreement, regional states will be skeptical about the convention's ability to effectively restrain Washington and Beijing.

these systems in coercive (if not necessarily violent) strategies to cost-effectively blunt Chinese escalation dominance or simply to defend what territory they still possess. Of course, this would generate wider problems for regional peace, undermining NDAA #2 and #3. Washington may have to enforce the US-China regime and other international agreements against its own security partners. Consequently, in pursuing an accommodation strategy, the US is betting that reducing Chinese assertiveness outweighs local disappointment to foster a durable settlement and regional peace.

This approach is the "cheapest" of the three options, as the US would not need to engage in an extended build-up of paramilitary coercive power to challenge the CCG and PAFMM symmetrically, as in both other options. Nor would it expend the long-term political capital needed to create a durable, comprehensive maritime settlement, as with the extended deterrence strategy. If this accommodation approach is structured and implemented carefully, Washington will have secured its central interest in freedom of navigation while potentially reducing the risk of future territorial conflict and off-loading maritime management tasks to Beijing. That said, this strategy carries at least three risks. First, it turns on the assumption that US acceptance of Chinese claims will end or substantially reduce Beijing's revisionism. This assumption could be wrong. China may possess domestic political and status-based reasons to continue pursuing revisionism even after accommodation. This option would then simply embolden the CCP to demand greater concessions from a stronger position. Second and relatedly, China may have time-inconsistent preferences. Even if accommodation successfully converts the CCP's current leadership into satisfied actors, once they have secured their maritime objectives, what incentive do they have to remain in a US-China agreement? As proposed above, the US could build specialized institutions to "lock in" Chinese compliance, or it could augment partners' military capabilities as a hedge. But if conflict does occur, the US would face significantly higher costs in forcing renewed access to the region. Those costs alone—and the consequent reduced likelihood of American intervention—may incentivize China to break the agreement. Third, it may not be possible to isolate this settlement from the broader US-Chinese relationship. Both sides may be tempted to link, say, trade disagreements to this accommodation strategy, exchanging concessions across issues. Paul Poast (2013) argues that issue linkage—specifically economic cooperation for military alliances—can increase the likelihood and durability of agreement. However, the current downward trajectory of

US-China trade relations suggests that linkage might pull both agreements apart. If a maritime settlement rests on resolving, say, trade tensions, this increases the chance of institutional failure and renewed conflict, again with China occupying a more advantageous position.

Moreover, an accommodation strategy would greatly damage US credibility among other regional states. Although accession to UNCLOS can ameliorate this harm, local countries would have significantly less reason to trust American declarations supporting a regional or even global maritime order. In particular, the US may have to walk back its recognition of *de facto* Japanese and Philippine control over disputed islands as part of its condominium with China, raising questions about American commitment to the respective MDTs. To partially mitigate this problem, the US could accommodate China only in the South China Sea. During the Scarborough and Second Thomas Shoal incidents, Washington never definitively stated that the MDT covers Philippine control of those territories. By contrast, the Obama administration clearly and repeatedly extended security guarantees to Japanese administration of the Senkakus. By agreeing to Chinese authority only in the South China Sea, Washington would avoid reneging on a direct promise to Tokyo and preserve the central American alliance in Asia. The benefits of such a policy, however, are limited. Even a partial accommodation strategy requires the widespread rollback of US neutrality to security and military partners like the Philippines, Taiwan, Malaysia, and even Vietnam. Likewise, Japan will be concerned that such actions signal future American unreliability towards its position on the Senkakus, given sufficient Chinese pressure.

Compared to the other options, this strategy carries the highest risk of catastrophic failure. It sacrifices—or indeed exchanges—growing regional support for US leadership to instead satisfy Beijing's demands. The US could hedge against Chinese violations by strengthening its ability to reenter the region and reinforce allies' naval and air forces. Indeed, this approach's military implications dovetail with current US threat perceptions and acquisition strategy. Accommodation cedes to China the paramilitary coercive domains essential to gray zone strategies. Rather than directly countering the CCG and PAFMM, the US denies those engagements and concentrates instead on the conventional weapons and preparations necessary for great power/peer competition. Successive US military strategies—such as Air-Sea Battle, the Third Offset, the Army's Multi-Domain Operations, and their successors—fit organically within this framework, given their focus on technological and operational superiority by conventional American forces. Investment in ISR, long-range strike, and power projection capabilities against Chinese A2/AD systems would be particularly useful in augmenting Japanese, Korea, and other allies' military strategies, which focus more on local defense. Further development of hypersonic weapons, unmanned platforms, AI, and big data analysis would provide the US with the surveillance, threat evaluation and prioritization, and strike capabilities to confront and defeat Chinese forces, enhancing some of the political and strategic options at Washington's disposal. Similarly, American withdrawal from the Intermediate Nuclear Forces treaty, while possibly unwelcome in Europe, allows the US to develop and deploy land- and sea-based missile systems that counter China's ballistic missile build-up over the past several decades. This approach can also encompass Krepinevich's archipelagic defense strategy. Under that plan, US ground forces take primary responsibility for or play critical contributing roles in ballistic or conventional missile delivery, missile defense, anti-submarine, and mine laying operations. As Krepinevich (2015) writes, "By shouldering greater responsibility for denying the PLA the air and sea control it needs to mount offensive operations, ground forces could liberate US and allied air and naval forces to perform the missions only they can accomplish, such as long-range surveillance and air strikes."

Washington can use selective force deployments to shore up regional alliances. However, a build-up in conventional arms does nothing to challenge or curtail Chinese dominance of the paramilitary coercive domain. Indeed, in the face of such an American conventional build-up, Beijing has even greater incentives to continue its gray zone strategy until and unless the US can craft an acceptable agreement. This of course increases the difficulty of accommodating in the first place. Most importantly, a conventional build-up elides the central political question: would the US really risk war against China by using military forces to escalate and resolve a territorial dispute in which it has only limited interests? Indeed, as the cases illustrated, Beijing's gray zone strategy is premised on exacerbating differences in interest intensity between the US and its allies. Only by possessing equivalent sub-military maritime forces or countermeasures against China's CCG and PAFMM dominance can Washington avoid that question. But the accommodation strategy is specifically premised on the US withdrawing from exactly this form of maritime competition with China, seeking instead a diplomatic and political solution. In addition, a military build-up will likely undermine Beijing's support for an accommodation strategy, as the US is specifically augmenting its ability to contest control over the South and East China Seas. Consequently, implementing an accommodation strategy will be challenging, not least because the military hedging required to assure local allies contradicts the stated objective of seeking and locking in Chinese cooperation.

Renewed Pivotal Deterrence

Key Elements:

- US develops and deploys paramilitary capabilities that can defeat or elide Chinese forces in the same domain.
- Washington reduces security commitments and military assistance programs to regain pivotal flexibility.

Of the courses of action, the renewed pivotal deterrence option best mirrors the United States' longstanding preference ordering among its Asian maritime objectives. Regaining a pivotal position requires significant US investment in paramilitary coercive capabilities, meeting the Chinese gray zone strategy in its own domain. Augmenting conventional forces, as with the accommodation strategy, would provide Washington with additional political and military flexibility in responding to future aggression by Beijing. As a result, this strategy will be more expensive in military and financial terms than the accommodation approach. But American dominance in these coercive domains would safeguard free passage and the territorial status quo for all vessels and states (NDAA #1). The US would avoid tying its policy to Chinese agreement, and it would reestablish the trilateral balance preventing both Beijing and Asian allies from unilaterally altering the territorial status quo. This should reduce regional conflict and deter coercion from any source (NDAA #2), without drawing the US into sovereignty disputes of secondary concern. With US preeminence once again (informally) backing UNCLOS, local states should more strongly adhere to international law and standards on American terms (NDAA #3). Critically, Washington could avoid US accession to the Convention, the better to preserve American freedom of action.

Building up military and especially paramilitary capabilities is the critical step in effecting this strategy. The CCG and PAFMM provide Beijing with cost-effective power projection, provided conflicts remain below the threshold of war. To overcome these forces without escalating, the US must develop, acquire, and deploy its own paramilitary systems.[22] In addition, Washington cannot match China's vast fleets with manned platforms and operations. Even with regional assistance, manpower shortages and intra-allied coordination problems would limit the size and effectiveness of this kind of response to a consolidated Chinese actor. Instead, the US should lean on its advantages in advanced technology, alongside select allies. Unmanned underwater, surface, and aerial vehicles can provide the ISR and strike capabilities necessary to locate Chinese vessels while reducing manpower costs. These units can use non-lethal but kinetic force to disable those units, by for example ramming or entangling propellers or propulsion systems. Aerial drones are particularly useful in an ISR role, but the US could also look into adapting these vehicles to carry non-lethal and/or counter-material munitions. Lockheed Martin is attempting to integrate microwave radiation weapons onto UAV platforms in a counter-drone role (Keller 2018). A similar system could be used to damage navigation, communications, and other sensitive shipboard electronic devices. With sufficient advances in miniaturization, aerial drones could be equipped with portable versions of the Active Denial System to target PAFMM and CCG personnel, or directed energy weapons like the XN-1 LaWS to disable engines and other critical systems. Even relatively simple, "low-tech" measures like firing pepper spray devices from UAVs could significantly degrade sailors' capabilities, prevent them from accomplishing missions, or drive them overboard (Carroll 2014).

Deploying such forces will demonstrate the United States' ability to challenge China *within* the sub-conventional domain, reestablishing a pivotal position. Controlling misperception and retaliatory escalation in such encounters will be critical, but, as several scholars find, states are less likely to make escalatory responses to military operations solely involving "drones" (Lin-Greenberg 2019; Schneider and Macdonald). In particular, the US Army and Marines can play a much larger role in this "drone-centric" strategy. They can remotely operate unmanned forces from forward bases or the US homeland, freeing Navy and Air Force units to pursue other missions. In addition, these ground forces can leverage their more extensive experience

---

22   Alternatively, the US could shift its redlines such that current Chinese operations will lead to open military conflict. That would likely embolden regional allies to launch their own incursions, hoping to entrap the US into a dispute and undercutting pivotal deterrence's central goal of preventing conflict from any source.

in non-lethal anti-personnel and counter-material munitions and weapons systems, leading to greater innovation about how to pair these systems with remotely operated crafts. By increasing the service branches, capabilities, and personnel the US can bring to bear, this approach would substantially complicate the Chinese strategy.

An acquisition strategy centered on unmanned vehicles to contest the sub-military domain suffers from several shortcomings. While these systems are certainly cheaper than conventional military forces, the larger and more capable underwater and surface crafts—like the Lockheed Martin Orca or Sea Hunter-class vessels—are still significantly more expensive than PAFMM trawlers. In an attritional engagement, China could impose an unfavorable loss exchange ratio. Cheaper vehicles, such as those based on the REMUS design, may not be able to catch up to PAFMM and CCG forces. The US could overcome this drawback by using airdrop capable units or investing in ferry platforms that transport and deploy cheap, short-range strike vehicles. The latter dovetails with calls to create "all-UAV carriers" (Shugart 2017). Moreover, the Department of Defense must address the sheer quantity of Chinese maritime forces as well. The US can certainly mass-produce "swarms" of aerial drones sufficient to match the CCG and PAFMM. But it cannot remotely pilot each of these vehicles. Instead, these platforms require algorithms allowing autonomous movement, coordination, targeting, and even firing authority. In addition to increasing unit costs and the expense of developing such software, these capabilities could violate emerging legal opinion on lethal autonomous weapons (Carpenter 2013; Docherty 2012; Horowitz 2016; Horowitz, Kreps, and Fuhrmann 2016). A final problem is the longevity of this strategy. The US Air Force and Army are both experimenting with anti-drone, area denial systems using microwave radiation to disrupt swarms (Cohen 2019; Pawlyk 2019; Snow 2018). China is rapidly developing similar capabilities (Huang 2018). As another counter-measure, Beijing could field its own unmanned units. This would increase the costs of their gray zone strategy but would allow them to deploy even more units and again shift the balance of forces against the US. Finally, as discussed in Chapter Two, a key component of China's gray zone strategy is ambiguity regarding escalation. Regional states worry that a Chinese fishing trawler could in fact be a PAFMM ship, providing Beijing with a pretext to deploy more capable CCG and PLAN vessels in response. China could use a similar strategy to stymie an American drone-based strategy. Mixing PAFMM and CCG forces with regular fishing trawlers would complicate US targeting, forcing Washington to accept the increased risk of mistakenly striking an official Chinese vessel and thereby escalating the conflict, at relatively little cost to Beijing.

A build-up of conventional forces can support—but not replace—expanding paramilitary capabilities under a pivotal deterrence approach. A key objective of gray zone strategies is delinking the military and paramilitary coercive domains. Practitioners attempt to find a step on the escalation ladder beyond which adversaries are politically unwilling to cross. So long as the US and its partners refuse to challenge China at the sub-military level, Beijing should be content to keep its coercive activity there. But China could react to the erosion or loss of paramilitary dominance by launching limited military actions. For example, the PLAN could take a more active role in situations like the HYSY 981 oilrig standoff, more clearly demonstrating its presence to deter further escalation by regional states. China's rapid increase in A2/AD and power projection capabilities provides additional layers of support. Deploying American strike capabilities—like anti-ship missile batteries—can blunt this response, forcing conflict back to the paramilitary domain. However, this would increase the risk of accidental or even intentional military combat between the US and China.

Separately, Washington must also decide what role allied forces can and should play in a renewed pivotal deterrence strategy. Perhaps the most critical lies in establishing and maintaining Maritime Domain Awareness (MDA). The US already benefits greatly from the ISR capabilities of Japanese, Korean, Australian, and other forces and their integration into US electronic surveillance and battlespace awareness systems. As an initial step, Washington could deepen and extend MDA cooperation to other security partners, like Taiwan and Vietnam, improving the speed and efficacy of American responses to Chinese incursions (Cheng 2019; Easton and Schriver 2014). An additional function lies in geography. Regional military bases would continue to serve critical logistics, maintenance, and intelligence functions. The sub-conventional forces necessary to the pivotal deterrence strategy will increase the need for forward-deployed operational command, supply, and repair services compared to current requirements. Allies can also host more conventional weapons supporting the pivotal deterrence strategy. For example, analysts worry that the US is falling behind in the race to create hypersonic missiles, which allow for rapid and long-range strikes that can disable critical parts of China's A2/AD network and facilitate the missions of more traditional US power projection forces. However, the Department of Defense could accomplish many of the same missions by deploying cheaper medium-range ballistic missiles across the "first island chain." Alongside sub-conventional systems performing ISR missions, these deployments would again reinforce US escalation dominance at a more favorable loss exchange ratio and thereby reduce Chinese gray zone incursions.

However, pivotal deterrence limits the depth of US-allied cooperation. The strategy benefits from allied operations that augment American capabilities and missions. But while seeking to roll back China's gray zone strategy, the US simultaneously wants to prevent renewed territorial acquisition by its security partners or regional states more generally. Consequently, it must avoid or alter activities enhancing these countries' ability to independently change the status quo. Training programs like the South China Sea Maritime Security Initiative or US Coast Guard Shiprider operations and combined military exercises—like Foal Eagle with South Korea or Keen Sword with Japan—enhance allied interoperability and operational effectiveness.[23] But Washington must ensure that participants are restrained from using these capabilities to escalate conflict with China. Similarly, under this strategy, US arms sales should focus on defensive—and not power projection—units. Washington should further emphasize multi-year supply and maintenance agreements as another mechanism to restrain security partners. Finally on this point, the US must also avoid allied misperception of American commitment to reduce entrapment risk. Japan or the Philippines could seize upon Obama administration promises that their respective MDTs cover contested territory to escalate disputes with China. Washington may need to privately or even publicly add conditions to those guarantees, exercise other policy levers to restrain Tokyo and Manila, or possibly walk back these declarations to prevent allied escalation. In total, this withdrawal of American security coordination will weaken the region's ability to jointly meet conventional Chinese challenges and will undermine US efforts to induce allies to take up a greater share of the security burden. But, for this strategy to be effective, the US must reserve command of pivotal

---

23   Information on the Maritime Security Initiative can be found at https://www.dsca.mil/programs/section-1263-south-china-sea-scs-maritime-security-initiative-msi. Information on the Shiprider program can be found at https://coastguard.dodlive.mil/tag/shiprider-program/.

forces for itself, limiting alliance coordination and securing the flexibility Washington requires to deter conflict from all quarters.

Achieving a stable balance between American military preponderance and allied caution is tricky. Pivotal deterrence requires the forward deployment of additional US equipment and personnel, given the limited range of unmanned platforms. Host states may believe this signals or implies greater American support for their positions than Washington actually intends. In addition, they will be increasingly targeted with deniable or covert attacks, such as cyber-intrusion, to probe US readiness and capabilities. These countries will demand compensatory American policy concessions and additional security commitments as the price of hosting this equipment. Existing security institutions can help manage these issues, but Washington must limit the clarity and scope of its promises to preserve the flexibility required for pivotal deterrence.

In adopting this strategy, Washington would halt the recent tilt towards closer American security cooperation by regional states. To be sure, rising Chinese capabilities and assertive foreign policies under Xi Jinping will continue driving local countries towards the US. However, Washington could leverage the current tilt to lock in regional leadership, as with the extended deterrence strategy presented below. Doing so, however, requires deeper and clearer American commitment to resolving territorial conflicts. Instead, pivotal deterrence prizes flexibility, particularly to avoid entrapment in secondary interests like Asian maritime sovereignty. Washington must forgo some of this momentum to preserve its policy independence. Regional states will still rely upon on US power: indeed, they have little choice. But lacking American adherence, local countries have fewer incentives to abide by UNCLOS guidelines and less reason to believe that international law will successfully adjudicate territorial disputes. Moreover, Washington will continue to lack the regularized communication and coordination channels UNCLOS provides to shape signatory behavior and interests, depending instead on its own network of alliances and informal security ties.

Overall, the pivotal deterrence strategy does not require a shift in US foreign policy and security goals, but rather investments that bring American capabilities in line with those objectives. Moreover, it provides a better hedge against continued or future Chinese revisionism than the accommodation strategy, as US forces can contest the sub-military domain. If successful, this approach will reestablish the power preponderance to also deter allied and security partner revisionism. Flexibility is the hallmark of the pivotal strategy. Rather than capitalizing on recent trends towards alignment with Washington, this approach foregoes that advantage, instead using threats of abandonment to avoid emboldening or being entrapped by allies. In short, this strategy assumes that medium-term risks of unwanted conflict outweigh short-term alignment gains. If that assumption is wrong, however, the following strategy—extended deterrence—can mitigate these risks through the use of institutionalized settlements and coordination of security operations.

Extended Deterrence

Key Elements:

- US leads a settlement process resolving sovereignty disputes among non-Chinese regional claimants.
- Washington establishes a political-military institution to buttress that settlement and resolve or respond to future violations.
- US attains primacy in military and sub-military domains against Chinese forces, incorporating regional allies/partners in response planning, operations, and support and readiness missions.

At its core, the extended deterrence strategy considers Chinese revisionism the greatest threat to American regional interests. While other Asian states have and may again establish outposts and reclaim marine land features, the scale of China's operations dwarfs these prior activities and particularly destabilizes the status quo. As discussed in the previous chapter, Beijing's policies have pushed Asian states towards the US. This presents a cautious opportunity for Washington to obtain all three NDAA objectives, but only if it is willing to elevate Asian maritime sovereignty issues to a core American interest and actively establish a durable settlement resolving them. In essence, the extended deterrence strategy contends that freedom of the seas (NDAA #1) requires a peaceful and comprehensive settlement of sovereignty disputes through the use of clear and commonly determined rules (NDAA #3). This will defuse regional conflict and deter Chinese coercion (NDAA #2). Under this approach, Washington trades deeper engagement on sovereignty issues for support for American leadership by Asian partners. That leadership will assure these countries of Washington's commitment to clarify and bolster maritime and territorial rules and will provide a focal initiative around which they can cohere. Regional buy-in to the agreement closes off the political gaps that China exploits in prosecuting its gray zone strategy. Furthermore, institutionalized arrangements provide partners a clear framework under which to consult and respond to future provocations. Ultimately, a political settlement of regional disputes is the linchpin to this strategy.

Extended deterrence assumes that China will not change into a satisfied, status quo-oriented power without the US first fostering political cohesion, common objectives, and coordinated policies among its Asian allies and security partners. But what if that assumption is wrong, as the accommodation strategy posits? Extended deterrence specifically opposes Beijing, would strengthen hardline voices in the CCP and Chinese government, and would weaken those pushing to work within the US-built network of political, economic, and security institutions. If the assumption is wrong, Washington could have secured Beijing's acceptance of international rules more cheaply and effectively through an accommodation or especially a renewed pivotal deterrence strategy. Moreover, given that maritime sovereignty issues are a core Chinese interest, Beijing can be expected to substantially reduce cooperation in other policy areas in response to this more coercive approach. The CCP's behavior during the current trade war suggests that it is willing to impose significant harm on its domestic economy and citizens in order to more effectively and extensively pressure the US through retaliatory tariffs and industrial policy (Fetzer and Schwarz 2019). Before pursuing an extended deterrence strategy, Washington must decide where freedom of the seas and maritime settlement rank in the wider portfolio of US-China relations. This decision is made easier since the extended deterrence approach aligns with the broader foreign policy and political trends. Both the US National Security Strategy and the National Defense Strategy (NDS) treat China as the country's primary strategic competitor, and there is a growing consensus among policymakers that US engagement failed to produce greater Chinese adherence to international rules, foster democratic governance, or encourage it to act as a "responsible stakeholder."[24] Within Southeast Asia, Beijing has leaned on countries like

---

24 A summary of the NDS can be found at https://dod.defense.gov/Portals/1/Doc uments/pubs/2018-National-Defense-Strategy-Summary.pdf. See Bader (2018), Campbell and Sullivan (2019), Dobbins and Wyne (2018), and *The Economist* (2018).

Cambodia to prevent an ASEAN response to its maritime activities. But this has generated significant policy differences among member states, particularly Vietnam, the Philippines, and to a lesser extent Malaysia. A US-led settlement initiative capitalizes on these divisions, engaging in "contested multilateralism" to provide an alternative institutional framework to manage sovereignty disputes, ideally linked to broader international regimes like UNCLOS (Morse and Keohane 2014). Sufficient regional cohesion may even induce Chinese membership, so long as Beijing demonstrates its willingness to comply with the settlement's terms. Membership acts as a screening mechanism, bolstering adherence to international law.

The extended deterrence strategy involves several, inter-related components:

- A political settlement of territorial sovereignty disputes;
- A standing security organization coordinating partner-US responses to future maritime violations and disputes; and
- Allied military assistance and combined operations programs.

The most important is the political settlement. China exploits divisions between East and Southeast Asian nations to fragment opposition to its maritime operations, weaken collective responses, and prevent US engagement. By resolving overlapping territorial claims and binding states to a common understanding of international maritime law, Washington reduces or eliminates these divisions, closing off gray zone challenges. The US need not abandon its neutrality on sovereignty disputes. However, it must lead the region by establishing a consultative and decision-making process and actively support the rules created. The Arbitral Tribunal's 2016 ruling serves as a legal guide for a potential settlement. It generally enhanced regional claimants' positions against China and underlined the utility and applicability of UNCLOS to these disputes. The US has also moved to embrace the judgment's contents (Cooper and Glaser 2020). While the ruling could serve as the kernel of a maritime settlement, the separate consultative and decision-making process will allow participants to create side bargains, such as joint development agreements, that go beyond the Convention and overcome legal obstacles. In addition, the process should fold in discussions over the proposed ASEAN-China Code of Conduct, strengthening what China prefers would be non-binding guidelines. Critically, the US should tie regional adherence to the settlement's provisions to the partner security assistance programs and coordinating institutions discussed below.

Importantly, this plan reduces American entrapment risks by giving Asian states less reason to return to revisionism themselves. A comprehensive settlement solves two strategic/negotiation problems. First, like other powerful states, the US has used bilateral negotiations and/or informal agreements to maximize its bargaining leverage and obtain better agreements. Multilateral discussions typically reduce these advantages. But they also expand the bargaining space, increasing both the range of benefits a settlement generates and the likelihood of successful agreement. In this case, a multilateral framework would better overcome Chinese attempts to create outside options and hive off regional support for a US-led agreement. For any individual dispute, Chinese local escalation dominance implies that the costs of American engagement outweigh the benefits, thereby deterring a US response. But a comprehensive, regional agreement would create larger and more widespread gains, including enhanced US leadership, a solidified block supporting American strategy against Chinese revisionism, and greater political cohesion that can be applied to other East and Southeast Asian challenges. The US could separately incorporate additional economic and diplomatic initiatives like a revived Trans-Pacific Partnership, further enhancing the benefits through issue linkage. In short, an "all or nothing" approach overcomes the prohibitive costs of engaging in each separate dispute by unlocking the externalities and gains from settling them altogether.

Second, regional states have ample incentives to participate in this scheme. Chinese maritime assertiveness has already led some to seek closer military ties to Washington. Existing institutions, most notably ASEAN, have manifestly failed to create a consolidated maritime security position among members, let alone leverage a united front to more effectively pressure China. Beijing has essentially split the organization by convincing Southeast Asian nations not party to the South China Sea disputes to exercise their vetoes within regional organizations. Washington's absence on these issues leaves accommodation with Beijing as the only viable option for many states. Countries like the Philippines settle with China, locking in mutually agreed but disadvantageous accords, a situation nevertheless preferable to "their current position of caving to Chinese intimidation" (Khanna 2018). If, however, the US engages in what Morse and Keohane (2014) call "competitive regime creation," it expands these countries' outside options and provides an alternative set of rules they can support. For the previous, pivotal deterrence strategy to succeed, the US must maintain a flexible posture. Washington's threats to withhold support restrains both China and American partners from revisionism. Under extended deterrence, by contrast, the US would secure partner compliance through attraction. Washington trades its policy autonomy and flexibility to instead bind partners to a commonly supported agreement that enhances US leadership and authority. This strategy takes advantage of recent Asian interest in closer security ties in response to Chinese aggression.

Lastly on the political settlement, US accession to UNCLOS would increase the likelihood of successful agreement. This idea was floated under the accommodation approach to reassure China about Washington's intentions. It can serve a similar function here, but oriented towards regional states. Indeed, accession would be even more meaningful for these weaker Asian countries than it would be for China, since they have less ability to challenge American maritime decisions outside of formal institutions. As previously mentioned, membership will tie US policy to internationally recognized rules. As the US Navy already follows the Convention, this represents little to no incremental cost for American forces. While legal concerns have prevented the US from joining, Washington can use the settlement process to supersede UNCLOS' provisions or carve out additional exceptions within the Asian maritime region. The costs of remaining outside UNCLOS rise as China coerces neighbors into following its preferred rules through its gray zone strategy.

The next component of the extended deterrence strategy is the creation of a standing security organization that coordinates partner-US responses to future maritime violations and disputes. Given the complexity of security and sovereignty issues in the South and East China Seas, the territorial settlement—no matter how comprehensive—cannot anticipate nor address all contingencies within the formal document. A political-military organization can serve as the locus for regional consultation about emerging maritime problems and coordinate joint policy responses to violations of the territorial settlement. This body need not include formal defensive guarantees like an alliance, nor be as extensive in scope as, say, the NATO Secretariat. Nevertheless, even a lighter institution serves critical policy coordination and adaptation functions, diminishing or foreclosing future political gaps that gray zone challengers can exploit. Membership will somewhat reduce US policy flexibility, but with active leadership, Washington can quickly marshal concerted, regional responses using the enhanced military and paramilitary capabilities discussed below.

Switching from a pivotal to an extended deterrence strategy involves a significant loss of bargaining power. Once the US aligns firmly behind its Asian partners, those states have less incentive to make further concessions. Consequently, when developing this security organization, Washington should leverage its temporary bargaining advantage to institutionalize favorable rules regarding burden-sharing; financing; force, material, and manpower contributions; voting or decision-making rules; command and coordinating authority; triggers for consultation; and information-sharing. This political-military institution is the primary mechanism by which the US will restrain security partners. Locking in US pre-eminence through institutional procedures and authority and reinforcing them through military-to-military ties (discussed below) is essential to reducing entrapment risks and to establishing actionable, coordinated agendas for maritime security. China of course is unlikely to assist in establishing this grouping. Even if Beijing expresses interest, its record of unilateral maritime revisionism suggests the US and its partners would be better served by first creating a "high-quality" instrument to which China can later accede (Gilligan 2004). Unless and until that happens, however, Beijing may attempt to fragment the agreement by picking off individual participants, as it has done in ASEAN.

For the extended deterrence strategy's final component, military transfers and cooperation flow from membership in both the maritime settlement and the political-military organization. Having screened member intentions and imposed institutional checks on their actions, the US can work to increase member capabilities with reduced concern about entrapment or partner revisionism. Of the courses of action offered here, the extended deterrence strategy requires the most US military investment, although this can be defrayed by allied contributions. This approach is one of American primacy. The US must possess the capabilities to contest and defeat Beijing in both military and paramilitary domains and support its allies in enforcing the maritime settlement. Enhancement of long-range strike and ISR capabilities, as envisioned under the accommodation strategy, would help ensure US access to the region against the Chinese A2/AD network, but Washington could rely more fully on local allies as staging and command nodes for medium-range ballistic missiles and unmanned forces, augmenting the early warning and detection systems already in place. Paramilitary forces would allow the US and its partners to meet the CCG and PAFMM symmetrically, disrupting the gray zone strategy.

But the most significant departure between an extended deterrence strategy and the two alternatives lies in the range and depth of US operational and even tactical coordination with partners and allies. Under an idealized pivotal deterrence strategy, the US retains command and control of coercive capabilities to enhance the decisiveness of its position and to avoid inadvertently emboldening allies. Under the current approach, Washington relies on institutional settlements to restrain misuse, reduce American burden sharing, and allow greater alliance coordination. Initial steps can include creating a partner-wide, integrated ISR and operational/tactical communications network to enhance MDA, coordinated logistics and supply systems modeled off of the Movement Coordination Center Europe, provocation and contingency planning, and combined military and sub-military exercises (Ross 2018). More aggressive measures can include joint patrols or, further, mixing national crewmen on certain patrol vessels modeled off the Coast Guard's Shiprider program. In addition to enhancing interoperability, this induces Chinese caution, as they must avoid unintentionally harming American service personnel. Admittedly, this raises the risk of direct conflict, but it clearly demonstrates US commitment and acts as "cost-effective" response achieving deterrence through only small operational adjustments.

The US should retain command and control of certain strike and defensive capabilities. Ballistic or guided missile systems, for example, could easily be misused by partners in operations against one another. But Washington can support allied deployment and use of sub-conventional systems. These include aerial and/or underwater drones used to defend individual ships or small fleets from PAFMM ramming or collision or, more assertively, to keep those forces at minimum safe distances. Moreover, US ground forces can play a much larger role in this strategy, reducing the burden on air and naval units. At forward bases on allied territory, they could perform traditional command and support roles for US missile platforms, early warning systems, and unmanned fleets and train allied forces in some of those capabilities. Land-based Army and Marine aircraft could assist US and partner navy, air force, and law enforcement operations. At the limit, soldiers can augment law enforcement operations at sea provided sufficient training in maritime interdiction and boarding. These would all address manpower and vehicle shortages incurred by relying upon more limited Naval and Coast Guard units (Cheney-Peters 2015).

The three components of the extended deterrence strategy—a maritime settlement, a supporting political-military institution, and allied/partner security assistance and cooperation—create gradations of cooperation, benefits, and responsibilities for Asian states. Those reluctant about political coordination and joint military training can still accede to the maritime settlement. But only by signing onto the political body will they have an institutional voice in managing future maritime challenges. Similarly, the US can scale its military assistance to regional states' level of involvement and response to US initiatives within that same political organization.

Conclusion

Extended deterrence is predicated on the US elevating the Asian maritime order to a vital interest. The global economic and political center of gravity is shifting toward the region, but it remains under-institutionalized relative to its financial and trade dynamism and to the magnitude of its longstanding and emerging security tensions. This strategy addresses that need and embeds American leadership. Extended deterrence represents a significant increase in the United States' security commitment, declared interests, and political engagement in Asia. Of the three strategies, this one is most likely to generate mission creep, the unintended enlargement of the policy's already expansive goals. Similarly, the strategy will create secondary and tertiary effects—both positive and negative—that states and international institutions must then manage. Finally, Beijing will retaliate, damaging existing US-China cooperation on many issues including terrorism, trade and international development, and global governance. Furthermore, China's ability to lean on economic and political levers—or example, the Belt and Road Initiative's massive funding potential—threatens regional state participation and adherence. Local countries would have both greater financial and economic ties to China and fewer resources with which to resist Beijing's pressure. Ideally, the US would couple its security strategy with a broader push for economic and even social engagement in Asia —for example, with a revived Trans-Pacific Partnership—to offset these Chinese benefits and provide regional states with a compelling alternative. But here already, buttressing the extended deterrence strategy expands US aims. The strategy lends itself to the US Department of Defense's (2018) "whole-of-government" approach to China's strategic rise. Consequently, in choosing an extended deterrence approach, American political leaders and strategists must be certain that Asian maritime security is and should be an integral component of a broader, multidimensional strategy. If not, then they should choose either accommodation or pivotal deterrence, where effort can more carefully calibrated to Asia's position within America's global interests.

More detail is needed to flesh out these individual strategies, converting the general recommendations made here into actionable proposals for specific service branches, allied militaries and statesmen, and the US diplomatic, international development, and public communications corps. But foundationally, the choice of Washington's response to China's gray zone strategy is a political decision. How does the value of US relations with regional states compare to that of the US-China relationship going forward? How important is confronting and deterring Beijing's gray zone strategy within the panoply of policy challenges and cooperative engagements facing the US and China? Given Xi Jinping's recent consolidation of power and the increasing salience of nationalist rhetoric over the past decades, is there still scope for Washington to shape Chinese incentives to become a status quo power? Regional states are waiting on the answers to these questions, and China will continue asserting control over maritime territory unless and until the US clearly coordinates a comprehensive strategy for East and Southeast Asia.

QUANTITATIVE ANALYSIS OF REVISIONIST
MILITARY COERCION, 1979–2001

Introduction

Chapter One focused our inquiry on a critical question: *what factors determine whether a state adopts a gray zone strategy and makes a moderately revisionist challenge?* Are gray zone challenges contests of initiative, driven by a revisionist's power and regional fragmentation?

This appendix uses statistical analysis to answer these questions, determining what factors systematically correlate with a state's decision to launch or avoid revisionist challenges. It allows us to control for variation in geography and time and exclude idiosyncratic variables that may have important effects in specific instances, but would mislead policy recommendations were we to generalize from those cases. In addition, as Goddard (2018) writes, revisionists have strong incentives to frame their actions as supporting the status quo (see also Goddard, Macdonald, and Nexon 2019), and they are unlikely to provide genuine justifications for actions altering the prevailing order. Following Skinner (1938), rather than analyze countries' statements to glean intentions, we instead assess their actions. Setting aside states' proclaimed justifications, what policies can states adopt that will invite or deter militarized revisionist challenges?

This appendix reaches three key conclusions. First, state type—whether a country is status quo- or revisionist-oriented—determines whether they make a gray zone challenge. Second, revisionist disputes are indeed contests of initiative, with target alliances and initiator power systematically deterring and driving challenges, respectively. Finally, gray zone challenges are not determined by a defender's power, as belligerents deliberately select targets and calibrate means to avoid directly confronting those capabilities.

The following section presents the data and methodology, all of which are commonly used in social scientific analysis. The appendix then describes the main models and their results and a variety of robustness checks. The penultimate section draws together analysis from across the models to discuss the statistical approach's overall implications for our understanding of the gray zone.

Data and Methodology

The principal data comes from the Correlates of War (COW) project, used extensively in political science and security studies research (Palmer et al. 2015). The models span 1979–2001 and include all countries in the international system. Since military threats and security cooperation are by definition relational concepts, the unit of analysis is the non-directed-dyad-year. That is, each possible pair of countries in each year enters the dataset as a single observation. By using this unit of analysis, we can assess the relative impact of military power, security coordination, financial resources, and other factors on the risk of coercive revisionism within these relationships. To operationalize "gray zone strategies," we use COW's Militarized Interstate Disputes (MID) data. This data records all instances of militarized threats, demonstrations of force (like military exercises), and direct conflict between conventional forces between two (or more) countries. Given Mazarr's (2015) focus on moderate revisionism, we are specifically interested in challenges threatening the status quo. Fortunately, MID includes a measure of each dyad member's status quo/revisionist orientation. Therefore, the dependent variable is a militarized, revisionist *Challenge*, a dummy indicating whether a revisionist state within a dyad threatens, demonstrates, or uses military force against a status quo country in that dyad in that year.[25] With a dichotomous dependent variable, we use logistic regression.

The dispositional nature of this paper's "gray zone" definition also affects how we operationalize the explanatory variables. We expect these variables to have different effects for revisionist versus status quo-oriented states. Expanded military capabilities, for example, should spur revisionist aggression, fueling conflict spirals. By contrast, we might expect status quo states to feel more secure, preventing those same spirals. Consequently, we must include both "revisionist" and "status quo" versions of each independent variable to gauge their separate effects. If, say, regime type (i.e., autocracy or democracy) possesses the same sign, significance, and magnitude in both versions, then state orientation (i.e., revisionist or status quo) has little influence on this variable. Note that this increases the book's analytical burden. The theory presented in Chapter One argues that initiative is the key factor driving gray zone challenges, specifically a revisionist's military capabilities and a target's embeddedness within security networks. The critical question is

---

25   For the remainder of this appendix, italics indicate a variable name.

which of these has a stronger, systematic effect. If, say, both the revisionist *and* status quo versions of military capabilities have the same effect on gray zone challenges, then this is evidence against any analysis that depends on a distinction between state types, like that in this book. If, however, those versions differ in effect, this highlights the importance of assessing state actions based on their adherence or departure from the status quo.

Table 3 summarizes the variables used in the models and our expectations for their effects. The key explanatory variables are a revisionist's coercive capabilities and the political cohesiveness between target states. To operationalize the former, the models employ the Composite Index of National Capability (*CINC*) index, a widely used measure of national material power developed by COW. This index aggregates six indicators—military expenditures; the number of military personnel, total energy consumption, iron and steel production, urban population, and total population—to create a single measure of national power. As mentioned, we expect higher levels of national power to spur military challenges by revisionist states, while stronger status quo countries should avoid such challenges.

Table 3: Theoretically Expected Effects on Likelihood of Revisionist Challenge.

VARIABLE	THEORETICALLY EXPECTED EFFECT ON REVISIONIST CHALLENGE	
	Status Quo	Revisionist
CINC	Negative, significant	Positive, significant
Alliance	Negative, significant	Sign ambiguous, possibly insignificant
Alignment	Negative, insignificant	Sign ambiguous, possibly insignificant
Polity	Negative, significant	Negative, significant
Major Power	Negative	Negative
Trade	Negative, significant	Negative, significant, larger effect than status quo version
GDPpc	Negative, significant	Sign ambiguous, possibly insignificant

For the latter concept, interstate security partnerships should bolster the political cohesion that stymies revisionist initiative. However, these partnerships come in many forms, each of which has different effects on the likelihood of gray zone incursions. Alignments are thinly institutionalized military relationships between states. Although they can include defensive guarantees, these partnerships lack detailed coordinating bodies and communication mechanisms. While an alignment between states indicates some common foreign policy positions, gray zone challenges deliberately test the cohesiveness of that connection. Indeed, these incursions intentionally subvert publicly declared redlines, and lacking regularized communication channels, partners should have difficulty developing collective responses. By contrast, alliances possess a coordinating organization or permanent bureaucracy (e.g., the NATO Secretariat or SHAPE). Compared to *Alignment*, these bodies are more heavily institutionalized and should provide members with robust, regularized means to respond to fluid situations and threats (Gelpi 1999; Haftendorn, Keohane, and Wallander 1999; Koremenos, Lipson, and Snidal 2001; Lipson 1991; Morrow 2000; Schroeder 1976; Wilkins 2012). Consequently, we expect the status quo version of *Alignment* to have little effect on revisionist challenges, while *Alliance* should have a strong deterrent effect. Each is a count variable measuring the number of alignments or alliances that a dyad possesses. Moreover, although less important for the analysis, the revisionist versions of these two variables have theoretically ambiguous effects on gray zone challenges. Revisionists with formal, institutionalized alliances can better coordinate with allies and succeed in their challenges. However, such states should be less likely to receive alliance offers in the first place, as partners would worry about entrapment and violating norms against territorial aggression. These same dynamics likely hold for revisionist alignments. But lacking extensive coordinating mechanisms, such partnerships are more susceptible to abandonment, potentially weakening revisionist's ability to successfully execute gray zone strategies.

I include additional variables to control for other factors that might lead to or dissuade revisionist challenges. *Polity* captures regime type, ranging from -10 (full autocracy) to 10 (consolidated liberal democracy). According to democratic peace theory, open polities are substantially less likely to go to war with one another. Moreover, democracies tend to win the wars they fight, and are better able to sustain conflicts over the long-term. All this suggests that revisionists are less likely to target democracies to avoid creating an implacable enemy. That said, open polities may be uniquely susceptible to hybrid warfare techniques, particularly propaganda, disinformation, and mass political manipulation. Their very openness allows gray zone practitioners freer access to media and to identify and exacerbate social cleavages. However, Lanoszka (2019) questions whether disinformation campaigns specifically have as large an effect as feared. The organized chaos of open politics and the organizing and screening functions of liberal institutions should blunt the efficacy of subversive operations. Taken together, democratic status quo states should be less susceptible to gray zone strategies, deterring their use. Consequently, this version of *Polity* should have a negative relationship to *Challenge*. On the revisionist side, autocracy may facilitate gray zone challenges by consolidating control of multiple policy tools under a single direction. With fewer public accountability mechanisms, authoritarian leaders may also suffer fewer costs from violating international norms against territorial or other forms of aggression. Like the status quo variant, revisionist *Polity* should also have a negative association with *Challenge*.

The models include a count for the number of major powers in the dyad, ranging from zero (no great powers) to two (both states are great powers). In the presence of *CINC*, *Major* captures the normative or legitimating qualities of international preeminence and power. Indeed, the original coders of this variable "designated them [as] 'legitimizers.'" These states establish the boundaries of acceptable behavior within the international system. Their approval or example confers legitimacy on particular policies, and their diplomatic recognition bolsters sovereign status (Krasner 1999). In short, great powers and their actions tend to define the international status quo. There are important limits to this claim. Conflict between great powers represents an ideological disagreement over international norms and the distribution of benefits (Haas 2005). The USSR established competing interstate institutions, regimes, and legitimating ideologies. Yet, within their respective spheres of influence, Russian and American actions performed similar functions, sanctioning certain behaviors and policies while prohibiting others. Moreover, within this paper's temporal scope, both the US and Russia followed general, if informal, rules of state conduct. Generally, we expect great powers to be status quo-oriented, and so *Major* should have a negative relationship with *Challenge*.

I also include two economic variables. *Trade* measures the total dollar value of imports and exports between the two countries in the dyad. According to Dorussen and Ward (2008) and Copeland (2000), increased trade flows should reduce the likelihood of conflict between states. Particularly given the explosive growth of goods and services exchange since the 1940s, warring countries sacrifice significant trade benefits if their economies are intertwined. Trade should restrain both revisionist and status quo-oriented states from conflict, and we might expect it to have a particularly strong effect on revisionists, who gain direct benefits from the prevailing structure of economic exchange. Indeed, insofar as China desires changes to the trading system, it is with the distribution of benefits and its position within that system, rather than the underlying trade rules themselves. Beijing has reaped significant financial and political gains from access to the international market. *Trade* should have a negative association with *Challenge*. Finally, I include *GDPpc*, the dyad's average GDP per capita. Gartzke (2007) finds that, much like democracies, capitalist countries are less likely to go to war with each other. It is harder for conquerors to expropriate goods and services from advanced economies, and richer countries have less reason to fight over resources, since those resources are less valuable compared to their existing economy (Angell 1910). Moreover, rich countries typically share common interests on a range of financial, trade, and even security policy, further reducing incentives to fight. Consequently, we would expect the status quo version of *GDPpc* to be negative and have a statistically significant effect on *Challenge*. That said, richer countries have greater ability to project power, and revisionist intentions give them reasons to do so. GDPpc might have crosscutting effects for these countries, and so there is no clear theoretical prediction about this version of the variable and the likelihood of gray zone incursions.

Results

Using these variables, the baseline model is:

Challenge =

$\alpha + \beta_1 (CINC \mid SQ) + \beta_2 (Alliance \mid SQ) + \beta_3 (Alignment \mid SQ) + \beta_4 (Major \mid SQ) + \beta_5 (Polity \mid SQ) + \beta_6 (Trade \mid SQ) + \beta_7 (GDPpc \mid SQ) + \beta_8 (CINC \mid R) + \beta_9 (Alliance \mid R) + \beta_{10} (Alignment \mid R) + \beta_{11} (Major \mid R) + \beta_{12} (Polity \mid R) + \beta_{13} (Trade \mid R) + \beta_{14} (GDPpc \mid R) + \varepsilon$

where is the intercept, "| SQ" and "| R" indicate the status quo and revisionist versions of the variables, respectively, and ε is an error term. I also include year fixed effects to further stress the model and account for unexplained heterogeneity across the interstate system.

Table 4: Model 1 Results. *Challenge* Includes Threats, Demonstrations, and Use of Military Force.

	Status Quo		Revisionist	
Intercept	-4.69	*		
	-0.45			
CINC	-0.61		154.70	*
	(11.74)		(10.85)	
Alliance	-0.26	*	1.46	*
	-0.07		-0.12	
Alignment	3.65×10^3		-0.23	*
	-0.03		-0.06	
Major	0.79		-14.61	*
	-0.77		(1.46)	
Polity	0.04		-0.65	*
	-0.03		-0.04	
Trade	8.41×10^6	*	-4.35×10^5	*
	(1.85×10^6)		(2.25×10^6)	
GDPpc	-4.35×10^4	*	2.51×10^3	*
	(5.1×10^5)		(1.14×10^4)	

N	224,596
AIC	1271.70
Residual Deviance	1199.70

* indicates significance at the 0.05 level using standard errors

Table 4 presents the results for this model. Beginning with the primary variables of interest, target state power has no effect on *Challenge*. As previously discussed, this is expected, as states deliberately use gray zone strategies to avoid or circumvent an opponent's strengths, especially military power. By contrast, revisionist capabilities are statistically significant, have a positive association with *Challenge*, and have a substantively large effect. In line with the theory, greater national power incentivizes revisionists to launch incursions against the status quo. Also following the theory, target *Alliances* strongly deter these challenges. The more embedded a state is in heavily institutionalized security partnerships, the more revisionists avoid them. This result is strengthened when considering *Alignment*, which has no systematic effect on *Challenge*.[26] It is close coordination that deters coercion, rather than having partners with common interests. Figure 2 simulates these effects as the number of formal alliances increase. The deterrent effect rises steeply until a state has nine partners, at which point the benefits remain generally constant. Note that the median state has eight formal alliances, putting such security cooperation within the reach of many countries. Interestingly, the signs for the revisionist versions of *Alliance* and *Alignment* flip. Informal security cooperation reduces the likelihood of gray zone strategies. As Benson (2012), Kim (2011), Morrow (2000), and Lipson (1991) discuss, states can easily renege on thinly institutionalized security commitments, as they invest fewer sunk costs and stake less of their reputations on fulfillment. This makes them less likely to launch revisionist incursions that can generate general, negative blowback. Those states with coordinated alliances, however, are more likely to initiate gray zone incursions, as they can efforts or prevent/blunt horizontal escalation by status quo countries. Furthermore, the "flipping" of these variables' sign and in some cases significance across status quo and revisionist versions suggests that states' satisfaction/dissatisfaction with the prevailing order strongly affects their willingness to launch gray zone incursions.

Turning to the other variables, the status quo versions of *Major* and *Polity* do not systematically affect revisionist challenges. Great powers and democracies are no more likely to receive threats or incursions than secondary states and non-democracies. In fact, the signs suggest that, were they significant, such factors would raise the risk of these challenges. By contrast, the revisionist versions of these variables are both statistically significant and negatively associated with *Challenge*. This aligns with the theoretical expectations for revisionists. Great powers favor the status quo and so are less likely to launch revisionist coercion. Similarly, democratic institu-

---

26 The sign is also positive, suggesting that informal security cooperation, were it significant, would increase revisionist challenges.

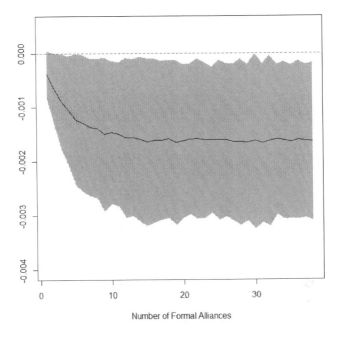

Number of Formal Alliances

Figure 2: Simulated Effects of *Alliance*. Shaded area represents 95 percent confidence interval. Note that, after four alliance partners, the interval never crosses the red, dashed 0-line, indicating statistical significance.

tions fragment executive authority, preventing revisionists from leveraging multiple tools of national power to pursue gray zone strategies. Here again, the status quo/revisionist distinction creates opposite effects on *Challenge*, further reinforcing Mazarr's (2015) approach. We see a similar "flipping" with the economic variables. Richer targets avoid revisionist incursions, but trade-connected ones receive them. Conversely, richer revisionists launch incursions, while trade-connected ones avoid them. Overall, revisionists better integrated into the international system—whether through status (*Major*), political norms (*Polity*), or economic exchange (*Trade*)— avoid issuing challenges to the status quo. By contrast, more powerful ones —measured through *CINC* or *GDPpc*—are more likely to initiate. Finally, the intercept is negative and significant, suggesting that states are strongly dissuaded from making revisionist challenges generally.

In Table 4, *Challenge* includes threats of military force. There is a rich literature on how states can make threats credible, particularly through the use of audience costs. But recent work shows how leaders can walk back escalatory promises while reducing domestic costs. Moreover, because threats are more numerous than demonstrations of force (like a military exercise) and direct military engagement, they could swamp the influence of these rarer observations.[27] Consequently, Table 5 restricts *Challenge* to only these two categories, examining the "high end" of gray zone incursions. The main variables of interest retain their signs and significance, changing only moderately in substantive strength. On the status quo side, *Alignment* and *CINC* continue to be insignificant, suggesting that power alone does not deter a revisionist challenge. *Alliance*'s substantive effect is weaker than in Model 1, as it is easier to align policy on threats when a challenger has clearly brought military forces into a conflict. Nevertheless, the variable remains significant and negative, again indicating that gray zone initiators tend to avoid states with coordinated security policies. Analogous to Figure 2, Figure 3 displays how alliance ties increasingly deter up to around fifteen partners. On the revisionist side, *Alliance* remains significant and positive, although its effect too is weaker, reflecting the greater risk involved in the demonstration and use of military force. Greater military power spurs gray zone incursions, as before.

Interactive Models

The results for Models 1 and 2 suggest that gray zone strategies are indeed contests of initiative. Revisionist power and target cohesion consistently predict the use of these strategies, and each has substantively large effects. Moreover, we can sharpen this analysis by using an interaction term. The previous models effectively treat *CINC|R* and *Alliance|SQ* as independent. Drawing upon Table 6 below, the result for *CINC|R* refers to the upper-left quadrant, where the revisionist state possesses significant coercive capabilities, which have a positive and systematic effect on gray zone challenges. Similarly, the result for *Alliance|SQ* refers to the lower-right quadrant. But the theory described in Chapter One suggests that these factors may be interdependent. When a revisionist challenger is powerful, but a target is also embedded in security networks, which has a stronger effect? If the former, then extending alliance guarantees and coordination will do little to deter incursions from powerful revisionists such as China. The US should instead attempt to erode Beijing's capabilities or match them with its own.

---

27 Including threats, only 0.296 percent of dyad-years (1015/342975) had a militarized dispute. The actual use of military force is even rarer, at 0.207 percent of observations (710/342975).

If the latter, then robust security coordination would be a key US policy lever. To preview the results, the models below suggest that the deterrent effect of alliances overwhelm those of revisionist capabilities, at least within the dataset.

Table 5: Model 2 Results. *Challenge* Includes Demonstrations and Use of Military Force.

	Status Quo		Revisionist	
Intercept	-4.78	*		
	-0.32			
CINC	-7.06		25.54	*
	-7.03		(7.39)	
Alliance	-0.16	*	0.45	*
	-0.02		(0.04)	
Alignment	-0.02		0.05	
	-0.02		(0.03)	
Major	1.14	*	-4.08	*
	-0.37		(0.59)	
Polity	0.07	*	-0.50	*
	-0.02		(0.02)	
Trade	4.91×10^6	*	-1.32×10^5	*
	(9.74×10^7)		(8.59×10^7)	
GDPpc	-2.27×10^4	*	9.64×10^4	*
	(2.75×10^5)		(3.35×10^5)	
N		224596.00		
AIC		3204.30		
Residual Deviance		3132.30		

* indicates significance at the 0.05 level using standard errors

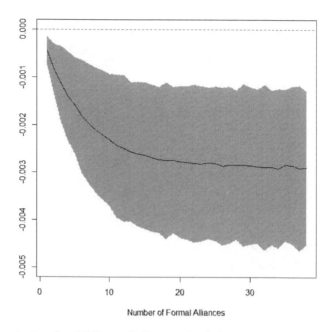

Figure 3: Simulated Effects of Alliance. Shaded area represents 95 percent confidence interval. Note that the interval never crosses the red, dashed 0-line, indicating statistical significance.

Table 6: Results from Model 1.

	Target Unallied	Target Allied
Revisionist Powerful	154.7 * (10.85)	?
Revisionist Weak	Null	-0.2607 * (0.04)

I rerun the previous analysis, but including a separate term—$CINC|R::Alliance|SQ$—multiplying the variables together. The results are substantively similar for most variables, and Table 7 and Table 8 focus on the theoretically critical variables in lieu of complete coefficient tables for brevity. Across both, powerful revisionists facing unallied targets are much more likely to issue gray zone challenges, particularly threats of military coercion. Yet, alliances eliminate this effect, as seen in the upper-right quadrants of those tables. Even strong revisionists are deterred from militarized challenges when a target cooperates closely with security partners.[28] As an aside, $Polity|R$ is negative and significant: the more con-

---

28 In addition to the tests presented here, I ran several robustness checks to verify the integrity and results of these models. First, international conflict is rare, and revisionist challenges even more so. Standard logit models, however, assume that events are reasonably common, at least 10 percent of observations. Consequently, I run a rare events logit method on all the models. The results are broadly similar to those reported here, with the primary explanatory variables (chiefly *Alliance*) possessing the same sign and significance and similar substantive effects.

Second, the models could be over-specified. Including too many controls could artificially inflate the significance of $CINC|R$ and $Alliance|SQ$. This is unlikely given the consistent results on these variables across all the models, but as an additional robustness check, I use "penalized" models (LASSO, ridge, and elastic net) to ensure that all variables are needed. For most models, one or no variables drop out. Moreover, the primary variables of interest survive in every case.

Third, initiative is modeled as a combination of target alliances and revisionist power. But would not a target's power augment the deterrent effect of its alliances? In other words, is the interaction term mis-specified, such that $CINC|SQ::Alliance|SQ$ is the correct variable? Replacing the previous interaction term with this new version, the model produces results in line with the theory. This new interactive term is statistically insignificant, although it does have the correct sign. $Alliance|SQ$ and $CINC|R$ retain their significance, signs, and substantive effects as well.

Finally, I conducted a set of additional tests producing problematic results. While the previous models assessed revisionist challenges from all state across two decades, this monograph is principally concerned with China. Does China respond to the same pressures as other revisionist actors? To answer this question using statistical methods, I replace $CINC|R$, $Alliance|SQ$, and $CINC|R::Alliance|SQ$ with "China-only" versions. That is, when China is the revisionist actor, $CINC|CH$ takes on its $CINC$ value, 0 otherwise. Similarly, $Alliance|CH$ is the number of institutionalized alliances a target state possesses when it faces a Chinese revisionist challenge. $CINC|CH::Alliance|CH$ is the interaction between these two new variables. These data contortions should isolate and test the effects of China-specific measures of initiative on *Challenge* and potentially reveal dynamics specific to Beijing's revisionism.

Unfortunately, this produces only 49 observations out of 224,597 following the breakdown below. With so few observations, models run on this data produce theoretically interesting results, but inconsistently. The variables of interest have different signs and significance in "regular" logit compared to rare events logit models, and these results are sensitive to how the measures are operationalized. Where prior robustness checks reinforced the models' results, on this data, they generate contradictory conclusions. For example, LASSO estimation recommends that the models drop $Alliance|CH$, and $CINC|CH::Alliance|CH$, while ridge and elastic net

solidated political authority is among revisionists, the more easily they can launch gray zone challenges.

Table 7: Results with Interaction Term. *Challenge* includes Threats, Demonstrations, and Use of Military Force.

	Target Unallied	Target Allied
Revisionist Powerful	176.8 * (14.7)	-12.01 * (0.98)
Revisionist Weak	Null	-0.19 * (0.04)

Table 8: Key Results with Interaction Term. *Challenge* includes Demonstrations and Use of Military Force.

	Target Unallied	Target Allied
Revisionist Powerful	62.69 * (7.47)	-3.28 * (0.37)
Revisionist Weak	Null	-0.13 * (0.02)

estimation suggest keeping those variables and eliminating *Trade|SQ* instead.

	Target Unallied	Target Allied
China Strong	25	9
China Weak	8	7

Instead of relying on further statistical methods to probe this final robustness check, Chapter Two uses qualitative case analysis to assess Chinese behavior specifically. As that chapter also supports the contests of initiative framing, this increases confidence in our theory by subjecting it to multiple, complementary tests beyond what one method can provide (Seawright 2016). The cases also have the advantage of extending our evaluation beyond the dataset's timeframe to 2015.

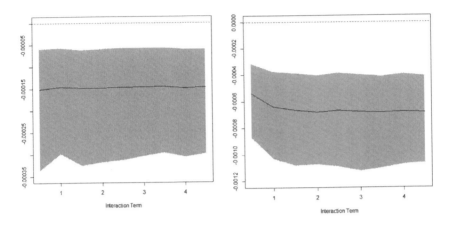

Figure 4: Simulated Effects of Interaction Term. Shaded area represents 95 percent confidence interval. Note that the interval never crosses the red, dashed 0-line, indicating statistical significance.

Statistical Implications for the Gray Zone

The models provide three overarching implications beyond the specific results detailed above. First, state type—whether a country is status quo- or revisionist-oriented—broadly determines whether it will make a gray zone challenge. The revisionist variables consistently obtained statistical significance across all the models, generally possessing the same signs and substantive effects. This contrasts with their status quo counterparts, where, for example, *CINC|SQ* and *Alignment|SQ* are never systematically related to *Challenge*. In addition, most variables' status quo and revisionist versions had opposing signs, further underlining the distinction. Taken together, this suggests that revisionism is a critical background or latent variable, supporting Mazarr (2015) in pinning his definition to this characteristic. It is also an inherently complex characteristic. While outside countries can affect a revisionist's preferences for conflict or cooperation, the process is indirect, and specific policies can have contradictory effects. For example, efforts to integrate revisionist states more deeply into the international economic system directly decrease the likelihood of challenges, but indirectly raise it by augmenting GDPpc and the ability to increase military capabilities. Efforts to induce status quo-oriented behavior among moderately revisionist states will achieve significantly less success than predicted given these complex interactions and recursive effects.

Second, the models provide strong support for the theory that revisionist disputes are contests of initiative. Target alliances and initiator power possessed the correct signs, significance, and substantive effects in all models, and these effects survived multiple robustness checks. While the US could try to directly or indirectly erode China's military capabilities, Washington may best shape Beijing's revisionist behavior by deepening security cooperation among regional states. Revisionists do not target the core military partnerships of the international system. Indeed, the use of gray zone strategies—and their reliance on deniability and escalation dominance—suggests this directly. They target peripheral countries lacking the ability to "internationalize" a challenge and thereby bring outside resources and pressure against a gray zone initiator. Alliance ties overwhelm the effects of even significant material capabilities, as the interaction models show. Moreover, "simple" military alignment between states is unlikely to deter gray zone challenges. Moderate revisionists target the "seams" of the international order: those issue domains and geographic areas where the robustness, institutionalization, and formalization of interstate agreement are thinnest. In addition, this analysis suggests that the more peripheral and less integrated a target state is to commonly agreed upon rules and institutions (and the less those institutions are backed by the military, political, and economic support of power states), the more militarized the gray zone challenge. Into these breaches, revisionists attempt to establish new rules, either by direct possession, the normalization of specific conduct, or creating new, replacement institutions.

Finally, gray zone challenges are not determined by the target's power. $CINC|SQ$ rarely obtains statistical significance, and this makes intuitive sense. Gray zone incursions are calibrated to avoid military responses, and so we might expect that target capabilities have less influence on *whether* it is challenged, as opposed to *how* it is challenged. Similarly, belligerents often possess greater capabilities, as proxied by $CINC|R$, meaning they are more likely to possess local escalation dominance. Consequently, enhancing a target's military power is by itself generally insufficient to deter revisionist challenges. To be sure, having capabilities at multiple levels or domains of conflict grants allies greater operational flexibility and the ability to contest a wider array of revisionism. But those partners must still confront several political/strategic questions: whether and when states and allies will use those capabilities, against what provocations, and to support what rules or to pursue what objectives. Allied cohesion and coordination are again essential to making those decisions, and creating, maintaining, or bolstering the necessary mechanisms among status quo-oriented states offers the best chance to foreclose the gains from initiative and halt revisionist operations.

Conclusion

This Appendix's statistical analysis affirms gray zone conflicts are contests of initiative. From 1979–2001, two factors—the target's alliances and the revisionist's power—systematically determined the effectiveness of these strategies. Importantly, the models also reveal that target power and informal security coordination have little effect in deterring subconventional coercion. Each of these results is robust to multiple statistical corrections and variable specifications, suggesting that the analysis accurately reflects the conflict dynamics at play.

Chapters Two and Three built upon the core insights of the quantitative models. This Appendix systematically mapped the relationship between our coercive and cohesive variables and the use of gray zone strategies. Chapter Two linked that broad analysis to specific cases. For example, the model results suggest that tightening alliances should decrease revisionist challenges. That chapter detailed Beijing's general pattern of deescalating tensions following declarations of US political and military support for Japan and the Philippines. Chapter Three then extended this framework to policy, outlining how Washington can create comprehensive foreign policy and military coordinating mechanisms under the extended deterrence option. Both chapters are grounded in the systematic analysis conducted here.

BIBLIOGRAPHY

Agence France-Presse. 2016. "Cambodia 'Blocking' ASEAN Sea Dispute Consensus." *Bangkok Post*, July 23, 2016. https://www.bangkokpost.com/world/1042597/cambodia-blocking-asean-sea-dispute-consensus.

———. 2012. "US Commander Reaffirms Philippines Defense Treaty." *Rappler*, April 22, 2012.

Altman, Dan. 2017. "By Fait Accompli, Not Coercion: How States Wrest Territory from Their Adversaries." *International Studies Quarterly*, 1–31.

Angell, Norman. 1910. *The Great Illusion*. New York/London, UK: G.P. Putnam's Sons.

ASEAN. 2014. "Foreign Ministers Statement." May 10, 2014. https://asean.org/wp-content/uploads/2012/05/24th-AFMs-Statement-on-SCS.pdf.

Associated Press. 1974. "China, Viet Rift Shunned by US." *Albuquerque Journal*, January 21, 1974. https://www.newspapers.com/clip/5952220/albuquerque_journal/.

———. 2016. "Philippines to 'set aside' South China Sea tribunal ruling to avoid imposing on Beijing." *The Guardian*, December 17, 2016. https://www.theguardian.com/world/2016/dec/17/philippines-to-set-aside-south-china-sea-tribunal-ruling-to-avoid-imposing-on-beijing.

Axe, David. 2019. "China's Secret Weapon to Control Its Near Seas: Enter the Maritime Militia." *The National Interest*, March 12, 2019. https://nationalinterest.org/blog/buzz/chinas-secret-weapon-control-its-near-seas-enter-maritime-militia-46837.

Bader, Jeffrey. 2013. *Obama and China's Rise*. Washington, DC: Brookings Institution Press.

———. 2018. "US-China Relations: Is It Time to End the Engagement?" *Brookings Institution*, September 2018. https://www.brookings.edu/

wp-content/uploads/2018/09/FP_20180925_us_china_relations.
pdf.

Beckley, Michael. 2015. "The Myth of Entangling Alliances: Reassessing
the Security Risks of US Defense Pacts." *International Security* 39 (4):
7–48. https://doi.org/10.1162/ISEC_a_00197.

Benson, Brett. 2012. *Constructing International Security: Alliances, Deterrence, and Moral Hazard*. Cambridge University Press.

Borger, Julian. 2014. "Putin Offers Ukraine Olive Branches Delivered by
Russian Tanks." *The Guardian*, March 4, 2014. https://www.theguard
ian.com/world/2014/mar/04/putin-ukraine-olive-branches-rus
sian-tanks.

Bower, Ernest and Gregory Poling. 2012. "Advancing the National Interests of the United States: Ratification of the Law of the Sea." *Center
for Strategic & International Studies*, May 25, 2012. https://www.
csis.org/analysis/advancing-national-interests-united-states-ratifica
tion-law-sea.

Bromund, Theodore, James Carafano, and Brett Schaefer. 2018. "7 Reasons
US Should not Ratify UN Convention on the Law of the Sea." *The
Heritage Foundation*, June 4, 2018. https://www.heritage.org/global-
politics/commentary/7-reasons-us-should-not-ratify-un-conven
tion-the-law-the-sea.

Calder, Kent, and Min Ye. 2004. "Regionalism and Critical Junctures: Explaining the 'Organization Gap' in Northeast Asia." *Journal of East
Asian Studies* 4: 191–226.

Campbell, Caitlin, Ethan Meick, Kimberly Hsu, and Craig Murray. "China's
'Core Interests' and the East China Sea." *Staff Research Backgrounder,
US-China Economic and Security Review Commission*, May 10, 2013.
https://www.uscc.gov/sites/default/files/Research/China's%20
Core%20Interests%20and%20the%20East%20China%20Sea.pdf.

Campbell, Kurt, and Jake Sullivan. 2019. "Competition Without Catastrophe: How America Can Both Challenge and Coexist With China." *Foreign Affairs*, August 1, 2019. https://www.foreignaffairs.com/articles
/china/competition-with-china-without-catastrophe.

Cardin, Ben. 2016. "The South China Sea Is the Reason the United States Must Ratify UNCLOS." *Foreign Policy*, July 13, 2016. https://foreignpolicy.com/2016/07/13/the-south-china-sea-is-the-reason-the-united-states-must-ratify-unclos/.

Carpenter, Charli. 2013. "Beware the Killer Robots: Inside the Debate over Autonomous Weapons." *Foreign Affairs*.

Carroll, James. 2014. "Vision-enabled riot control UAV fires pepper spray balls, communicates with crowds." *Vision Systems*, June 19, 2014. https://www.vision-systems.com/non-factory/article/16746110/visionenabled-riot-control-uav-fires-pepper-spray-balls-communicates-with-crowds.

Carson, Austin. 2016a. "Facing Off and Saving Face: Covert Intervention and Escalation Management in the Korean War." *International Organization* 70: 103–31. https://doi.org/10.1017/S0020818315000284.

———. 2016b. "Facing Off and Saving Face: Covert Intervention and Escalation Management in the Korean War." *International Organization* 70: 103–31.

Carson, Austin, and Keren Yarhi-Milo. 2017. "Covert Communication: The Intelligibility and Credibility of Signaling in Secret." *Security Studies* 26 (1): 124–56. https://doi.org/10.1080/09636412.2017.1243921.

Cesa, Marco. 2010. *Allies Yet Rivals*. Stanford University Press.

Cheney-Peters, Scott. 2015. "Joint Patrols and US Coast Guard Capacity." *Asia Maritime Transparency Initiative*, April 1, 2015. https://amti.csis.org/joint-patrols-and-u-s-coast-guard-capacity/.

Cheng, Dean. 2019. "The Importance of Maritime Domain Awareness for the Indo–Pacific Quad Countries." *The Heritage Foundation*, March 6, 2019. https://www.heritage.org/global-politics/report/the-importance-maritime-domain-awareness-the-indo-pacific-quad-countries.

Cherry, R.G. 1921. "The Initiative in War." *Royal United Services Institution Journal* 66 (461): 87. https://www.tandfonline.com/doi/abs/10.1080/03071842109421936?journalCode=rusi19.

Chubb, Andrew. 2015. "The South China Sea: Defining the "Status Quo.""

The Diplomat, June 11, 2015. https://thediplomat.com/2015/06/the-south-china-sea-defining-the-status-quo/.

Cohen, Rachel. 2019. "Microwave Weapons Moving Toward Operational Use." *Air Force Magazine*, March 20, 2019. http://www.airforcemag.com/Features/Pages/2019/March%202019/Microwave-Weapons-Moving-Toward-Operational-Use.aspx.

Cooper, Zack, and Bonnie Glaser. 2020. "What Options are on the Table in the South China Sea?" *War on the Rocks*. https://warontherocks.com/2020/07/what-options-are-on-the-table-in-the-south-china-sea/.

Cooper, Zack, and Gregory Poling. 2019. "America's Freedom of Navigation Operations are Lost at Sea." *Foreign Policy*, January 8, 2019. https://foreignpolicy.com/2019/01/08/americas-freedom-of-navigation-operations-are-lost-at-sea/.

Copeland, Dale C. 2000. "Trade Expectations and the Outbreak of Peace: Detente 1970-74 and the End of the Cold War 1985-91." In *Power and the Purse: Economic Statecraft, Interdependence, and National Security*. Edited by Jean-Marc F. Blanchard, Edward D. Mansfield, and Norrin M Ripsman. London, UK/Portland, OR: Frank Cass.

Cormac, Rory, and Richard J. Aldrich. 2018. "Grey Is the New Black: Covert Action and Implausible Deniability." *International Affairs* 94 (3): 477–94. https://doi.org/10.1093/ia/iiy067.

Crawford, Timothy. 2001-2002. "Pivotal Deterrence and the Kosovo War: Why the Holbrooke Agreement Failed." *Political Science Quarterly* 116 (4): 499–523.

———. 2003. *Pivotal Deterrence: Third-Party Statecraft and the Pursuit of Peace*. Cornell University Press.

Denyer, Simon. 2106. "US 'hypocrisy' and Chinese cash strengthen Beijing's hand in South China Sea." *The Washington Post*, June 19, 2016. https://www.washingtonpost.com/world/asia_pacific/us-hypocrisy-and-chinese-cash-strengthen-beijings-hand-in-south-china-sea/2016/06/18/6907943a-330a-11e6-ab9d-1da2b0f24f93_story.html?utm_term=.217a6b7b2b37.

Dobbins, James, and Ali Wyne. 2018. "Engagement vs. Competition: The China Policy Debate." *The Hill*, December 30, 2018. https://www.rand.org/blog/2018/12/engagement-vs-competition-the-china-policy-debate.html.

Docherty, Bonnie. 2012. *Losing Humanity: The Case Against Killer Robots*. Human Rights Watch. https://www.hrw.org/report/2012/11/19/losing-humanity/case-against-killer-robots

Dorussen, Han, and Hugh Ward. 2008. "Intergovernmental Organizations and the Kantian Peace: A Network Perspective." *Journal of Conflict Resolution* 52 (2).

Dutton, Peter. 2014. "China's Maritime Disputes in the East and South China Seas." *Naval War College Review* 67 (3): 2.

———. 2015. "China's Claims are Unambiguously Ambiguous." *Asia Maritime Transparency Initiative*, June 16, 2015. https://amti.csis.org/chinas-claims-are-unambiguously-ambiguous/.

Easton, Ian, and Randall Schriver. 2014. "Standing Watch: Taiwan and Maritime Domain Awareness in the Western Pacific." *Project 2049*, December 2014. https://project2049.net/wp-content/uploads/2018/06/141216_Taiwan_Maritime_Domain_Awareness_Easton_Schriver.pdf.

Echevarria, Antulio. 2016. *Operating in the Gray Zone: An Alternative Paradigm for US Military Strategy*. (Strategic Studies Institute.) Carlisle, PA: US Army War College. https://apps.dtic.mil/dtic/tr/fulltext/u2/1013691.pdf.

The Economist. 2018. "The End of Engagement." October 18, 2018. https://www.economist.com/leaders/2018/10/18/the-end-of-engagement.

Erickson, Andrew. "China Open Source Example: Shipyard Details Sansha Maritime Militia Vessel with 'Weapons and Equipment Room' (武备库) and 'Ammunition Store' (弹药库)." *China Analysis from Original Sources* 以第一手资料研究中国, March 24, 2017. https://www.andrewerickson.com/2017/03/china-open-source-example-shipyard-details-sansha-maritime-militia-vessel-with-weapons-and-equipment-room-and-ammunition-store/.

Erickson, Andrew, Joshua Hickey, and Henry Holst. 2019. "Surging Second Sea Force: China's Maritime Law Enforcement Forces, Capabilities, and Future in the Gray Zone and Beyond." *Naval War College Review* 72 (2).

Erickson, Andrew, and Conor Kennedy. 2015. "China's Daring Vanguard: Introducing Sanya City's Maritime Militia." *Center for International Maritime Security*, November 5, 2015. http://cimsec.org/chinas-daring-vanguard-introducing-sanya-citys-maritime-militia/19753.

Erickson, Andrew, and Ryan Martinson, eds. 2019. *China's Maritime Gray Zone Operations*. Annapolis: Naval Institute Press.

Fetzer, Thiemo, and Carlo Schwarz. 2019. "Tariffs and Politics: Evidence from Trump's Trade Wars." *CESifo Working Paper No. 7553*. https://papers.ssrn.com/sol3/papers.cfm?abstract_id=3357130.

Fravel, M. Taylor. 2011. "China's Strategy in the South China Sea." *Contemporary Southeast Asia* 33 (3): 292. https://doi.org/10.1355/cs33-3b.

Fuell, Lee. 2014. "Testimony before the US-China Economic & Security Review Commission." January 30, 2014. https://www.uscc.gov/sites/default/files/USCC%20Hearing%20Transcript%20-%20January%2030%202014.pdf.

Gartzke, Erik. 2007. "The Capitalist Peace." *American Journal of Political Science* 51 (1): 166–91.

Gelpi, Christopher. 1999. "Alliances as Instruments of Intra-Allied Control." In *Imperfect Unions: Security Institutions Across Time and Space*. Edited by Helga Haftendorn, Robert O. Keohane, and Celeste A. Wallander. Oxford: Oxford University Press.

Gilady, Lilach. 2018. *The Price of Prestige*. Chicago: University of Chicago Press.

Gilli, Andrea, and Mauro Gilli. 2016. "The Diffusion of Drone Warfare? Industrial, Organizational and Infrastructural Constraints: Military Innovations and the Ecosystem Challenge." *Security Studies* 25 (1).

Gilligan, Michael. 2004. "Is There a Broader-Deeper Trade-off in International Multilateral Agreements?" *International Organization* 58 (3): 459–84.

Glenn, Russell. "Thoughts on 'Hybrid Conflict.'" *Small Wars Journal*. March 2, 2009. https://smallwarsjournal.com/blog/journal/docs-temp/18 8-glenn.pdf.

GlobalSecurity.org. "China's Defense Budget." Last accessed Nov. 24, 2020. https://www.globalsecurity.org/military/world/china/budget-table. htm.

Goddard, Stacie. 2018. *When Right Makes Might: Rising Powers and World Order*. Ithaca: Cornell University Press.

Goddard, Stacie E., Paul K. Macdonald, and Daniel H. Nexon. 2019. "Repertoires of Statecraft: Instruments and Logics of Power Politics." *International Relations* 33 (2): 304–21. https://doi.org/10.1177/004 7117819834625.

Green, Michael, Kathleen Hicks, Zack Cooper, John Schaus, and Jake Douglas. 2017. Countering Coercion in Maritime Asia. *CSIS*. https:// www.csis.org/analysis/countering-coercion-maritime-asia.

Grossman, Derek, and Logan Ma. 2020. "A Short History of China's Fishing Militia and What It may Tell Us." *RAND Blog*. https://www.rand. org/blog/2020/04/a-short-history-of-chinas-fishing-militia-and-what.html.

Haas, Mark. 2005. *The Ideological Origins of Great Power Politics, 1789–1989*. Ithaca: Cornell University Press.

Haftendorn, Helga, Robert Keohane, and Celeste Wallander, eds. 1999. *Imperfect Unions: Security Institutions over Time and Space*. New York: Oxford University Press.

Halliden, Brian John. 2014. "China's Historic Rights in the South China Sea: A Time for Reconsideration and Pacific Settlement." Masters of Law Thesis, Naval Postgraduate School. https://calhoun.nps.edu/handle/10945/43070.

Headquarters, Department of the Army. 2011. "ADP3-0: Unified Land Operations." https://www.army.mil/e2/rv5_downloads/info/refer ences/ADP_3-0_ULO_Oct_2011_APD.pdf.

Heginbotham, Eric, Michael Nixon, Forrest Morgan, Jacob Heim, Jeff Hagen, Sheng Tao Li, Jeffrey Engstrom, et al. 2017. "US-China Military

Scorecard: Forces, Geography, and the Evolving Balance of Power, 1996–2017." https://www.rand.org/pubs/research_reports/RR392. html.

Hoffman, Frank. 2012. "Hybrid vs . Compound War: The Janus Choice." *Armed Forces Journal*, vol. 14. October 2009.

Horowitz, Michael. 2016. "The Ethics and Morality of Robotic Warfare: Assessing the Debate over Autonomous Weapons." *Daedalus*, 25–36.

Horowitz, Michael, Sarah Kreps, and M. Fuhrmann. 2016. "Separating Fact from Fiction in the Debate over Drone Proliferation." *International Security* 41 (2).

Hsu, S. Philip. 2010. "Reappraising the Debate and Practice of US Strategic Ambiguity/Clarity in Cross-Strait Relations." *The Pacific Review* 23 (2).

Huang, Kristin. 2018. "China in race for Counter-Drone Tech and Laser Weapons as It Tries to Catch up with US." *South China Morning Post*, August 25, 2018. https://www.scmp.com/news/china/diplomacy-defence/article/2161331/china-race-counter-drone-tech-and-laser-weapons-it.

Hunt, Katie, Matt Rivers, and Catherine Shoichet. 2016. "In China, Duterte Announces Split with US: 'America has Lost.' *CNN*, October 20, 2016. https://www.cnn.com/2016/10/20/asia/china-philippines-duterte-visit/index.html.

Hunzeker, Michael, and Alexander Lanoszka. 2018. *A Question of Time*. Center for Security Policy Studies, Schar School of Policy and Government. Arlington: George Mason University.

Huth, Paul. 1988. "Extended Deterrence and the Outbreak of War." *American Political Science Review* 82 (2): 424.

Ikenberry, G John. 2001. *After Victory: Institutions, Strategic Restraint, and The Rebuilding of Order After Major Wars*. Princeton, NJ: Princeton University Press.

Japanese Ministry of Foreign Affairs. 2019. "Trends in Chinese Government and Other Vessels in the Waters Surrounding the Senkaku Islands, and Japan's Response." July 9, 2019. https://www.mofa.go.jp/region/page23e_000021.html.

Japan Times. 2013. "China Officially Labels Senkakus a 'Core Interest.'" April 27, 2013. https://www.japantimes.co.jp/news/2013/04/27/national/china-officially-labels-senkakus-a-core-interest/#.UX5n Hcpv6zk.

Jennings, Ralph. 2019. "China Expected to Keep Its Exact Claim to Disputed Sea a Secret." *Voice of America*, April 5, 2019. https://www.voanews.com/east-asia/china-expected-keep-its-exact-claim-disputed-sea-secret.

Khanna, Parag. 2018. "South China Sea disputes must be Resolved through Arbitration that Seeks Mutual Benefit." *South China Morning Post*, July 23, 2018. https://www.scmp.com/comment/insight-opinion/united-states/article/2156193/south-china-sea-disputes-must-be-resolved.

Kapusta, Philip. 2015. "The Gray Zone." *Special Warfare* Oct.-Dec.

Keller, John. 2018. "Army Asks Lockheed Martin to Develop UAV High-Power Microwave Weapons to Destroy or Disable Enemy Drones." *Military & Aerospace Electronics*, August 6, 2018. https://www.militaryaerospace.com/unmanned/article/16726480/army-asks-lockheed-martin-to-develop-uav-highpower-microwave-weapons-to-destroy-or-disable-enemy-drones.

Kennedy, Conor, and Andrew Erickson. 2016. "Riding a New Wave of Professionalization and Militarization: Sansha City's Maritime Militia." *Center for International Maritime Security*. September 1, 2016. http://cimsec.org/riding-new-wave-professionalization-militarization-sansha-citys-maritime-militia/27689.

Kim, Tongfi. 2011. "Why Alliances Entangle But Seldom Entrap States." *Security Studies* 20 (3): 350–77.

Koremenos, Barbara, Charles Lipson, and Duncan Snidal. 2001. "The Rational Design of International Institutions." *International Organization* 55 (4): 761–99.

Krasner, Stephen D. 1999. *Sovereignty: Organized Hypocrisy*. Princeton, NJ: Princeton University Press.

Krepinevich, Andrew. 2015. "How to Deter China." *Foreign Affairs*. March/April. https://www.foreignaffairs.com/articles/china/2015-02-16/how-deter-china

Kreuzer, Peter. 2016. "A Comparison of Malaysian and Philippine Responses to China in the South China Sea." *Chinese Journal of International Politics* 9 (3): 239–76. https://doi.org/10.1093/cjip/pow008.

Kyodo News. 2016. "Malaysia, Singapore, Indonesia React to S. China Sea Ruling," *ABS-CBN News*, July 13, 2016. https://news.abs-cbn.com/overseas/07/13/16/malaysia-singapore-indonesia-react-to-s-china-sea-ruling.

Lague, David, and Benjamin Kang Lim. 2019. "The China Challenge." *Reuters Investigates*, April 30, 2019. https://www.reuters.com/investigates/special-report/china-army-navy/.

Lally, Kathy. 2014. "Putin's Remarks Raise Fears of Future Moves against Ukraine." *The Washington Post*, April 17, 2014. https://www.washingtonpost.com/world/putin-changes-course-admits-russian-troops-were-in-crimea-before-vote/2014/04/17/b3300a54-c617-11e3-bf7a-be01a9b69cf1_story.html?utm_term=.34e28fc06875.

Lan, Ngo Di. 2018. "The Usefulness of 'Redundant' Freedom of Navigation Operations." *Asia Maritime Transparency Initiative*, January 26, 2018. https://amti.csis.org/usefulness-redundant-fonops/.

Lanoszka, Alexander. 2016. "Russian Hybrid Warfare and Extended Deterrence in Eastern Europe." *International* Affairs. 92:1: 175–95.

———. 2019. "Disinformation in International Politics." *European Journal of International Security* 4 (2): 227–48. https://doi.org/10.1017/eis.2019.6.

Lee, John. 2016. "What Now for China's 'Historic Rights' in the South China Sea." *The Diplomat*, August 2, 2016. https://thediplomat.com/2016/08/what-now-for-chinas-historic-rights-in-the-south-china-sea/.

Lema, Karen, and Martin Perry. 2018. "Two Years after Philippines' Pivot, Duterte Still Waiting on China Dividend." *Reuters*, November 18, 2018. https://www.reuters.com/article/us-philippines-china-analysis

/two-years-after-philippines-pivot-duterte-still-waiting-on-china-dividend-idUSKCN1NN0UO.

Li, Cheng, and Lucy Xu. 2014. "Chinese Enthusiasm and American Cynicism Over the 'New Type of Great Power Relations.'" *Brookings Institution*, December 4, 2014. https://www.brookings.edu/opinions/chinese-enthusiasm-and-american-cynicism-over-the-new-type-of-great-power-relations/.

Liff, Adam. 2019. "China's Maritime Gray Zone Operations in The East China Sea and Japan's Response." In *China's Maritime Gray Zone Operations*. Edited by Andrew Erickson and Ryan Martinson. Annapolis: Naval Institute Press.

Lin-Greenberg, Erik. 2019. "Game of Drones: What Experimental Wargames Reveal About Drones and Escalation." *War on the Rocks*, January 10, 2019. https://warontherocks.com/2019/01/game-of-drones-what-experimental-wargames-reveal-about-drones-and-escalation/.

Lipson, Charles. 1991. "Why are Some International Agreements Informal?" *International Organization* 45: 495–538.

Litwak, Robert. 2012. *Outlier States: American Strategies to Change, Contain, and Engage Regimes*. Washington, DC: Woodrow Wilson Center Press.

Locklear, Admiral Samuel J. 2012. "Statement of Admiral Samuel J. Locklear: The Law of the Sea Convention: Perspectives from the US Military." Testimony before the Senate Foreign Relations Committee, June 14, 2012. https://www.armed-services.senate.gov/imo/media/doc/Locklear_04-16-15.pdf.

Mazarr, Michael. 2015. *Mastering the Gray Zone: Understanding a Changing Era of Conflict*. Strategic Studies Institute. Carlisle, PA: US Army War College. https://publications.armywarcollege.edu/pubs/2372.pdf

Mehta, Aaron. 2015. "Carter: China 'Out of Step' With Pacific." *Defense News*, May 29, 2015. https://www.defensenews.com/2015/05/30/carter-china-out-of-step-with-pacific/.

Mitchell, A. Wess, and Jakub Grygiel. "'Salami Slicing' and Deterrence." *The*

American Interest. November 18, 2014. https://www.the-american-interest.com/2014/11/18/salami-slicing-and-deterrence/

Moore, John Norton. 2004. "Testimony before the House Committee on International Relations." May 12, 2004. https://colp.virginia.edu/sites/colp.virginia.edu/files/house-testimony.pdf.

Morrow, James D. 2000. "Alliances: Why Write Them Down?" *Annual Review of Political Science* 3: 63–83.

Morse, Julia, and Robert Keohane. 2014. "Contested Multilateralism." *The Review of International Organizations* 9 (4).

Mourdoukoutas, Panos. 2019a. "China Wants to Apply the Duterte Model to Settle South China Sea Disputes with Malaysia." *Forbes*, May 23, 2019. https://www.forbes.com/sites/panosmourdoukoutas/2019/05/23/china-wants-to-apply-the-duterte-model-to-settle-south-china-sea-disputes-with-malaysia/#561e9be04b3e.

———. 2019b. "Philippines is Beginning to Pay the Price for Duterte's South China Sea Flip-Flops." *Forbes*, April 6, 2019. https://www.forbes.com/sites/panosmourdoukoutas/2019/04/06/philippines-is-beginning-to-pay-the-price-for-dutertes-south-china-sea-flip-flops/.

Murray, Williamson, and Peter Mansoor. 2012. *Hybrid Warfare: Fighting Complex Opponents from the Ancient World to the Present*. Cambridge, UK: Cambridge University Press.

Nemeth, William. 2002. "Future War and Chechnya: A Case for Hybrid Warfare." (MA Thesis). Monterey: Naval Postgraduate School. https://calhoun.nps.edu/bitstream/handle/10945/5865/02Jun_Nemeth.pdf?sequence=1&isAllowed=y

Oshima, Takashi, and Kenji Minemura. 2012. "Panetta Tells China that Senkakus under Japan-US Security Treaty." *Asahi Shimbun*, September 21, 2012.

Palmer, Glenn, Vito D'Orazio, Michael Kenwick, and Matthew Lane. 2015. "The MID4 Data Set: Procedures, Coding Rules, and Description." *Conflict Management and Peace Science*. 32 (2): 222–42.

Pan, Zhongqi. 2003. "US Taiwan Policy of Strategic Ambiguity: A Dilemma of Deterrence." *Journal of Contemporary China* 12 (35).

Panda, Ankit. 2018. "China Condemns US FONOP Near Mischief Reef in the South China Sea." *The Diplomat*, March 25, 2018. https://thediplomat.com/2018/03/china-condemns-us-fonop-near-mischief-reef-in-the-south-china-sea/.

Parameswaran, Prashanth. 2016. "Indonesia to Respond After South China Sea Case: Minister." *The Diplomat*, March 31, 2016. https://thediplomat.com/2016/03/indonesia-to-respond-after-south-china-sea-case-minister/.

Pawlyk, Oriana. 2019. "Air Force's Mjölnir? Service Testing THOR Anti-Drone System." *Military.com*, April 25, 2019. https://www.military.com/daily-news/2019/04/25/air-forces-mjolnir-service-testing-thor-anti-drone-system.html.

Pempel, T.J. 2010. "Soft Balancing, Hedging, and Institutional Darwinism: The Economic-Security Nexus and East Asian Regionalism." *Journal of East Asian Studies* 10: 209–38.

Phuong, Nguyen The. 2020. "Vietnam's Maritime Militia is not a Black Hole in the South China Sea." *Asia Maritime Transparency Initiative Update*, May 22, 2020. https://amti.csis.org/vietnams-maritime-militia-is-not-a-black-hole-in-the-south-china-sea/.

Pinsker, Roy. 2003. "Drawing a Line in the Taiwan Strait: 'Strategic Ambiguity' and Its Discontents." *Australian Journal of International Affairs* 57 (2).

Poast, Paul. 2013. "Issue Linkage and International Cooperation: An Empirical Investigation." *Conflict Management and Peace Science* 30 (3): 286–303. https://doi.org/10.1177/0738894213484030.

Pompeo, Michael. 2020. "US Position on Maritime Claims in the South China Sea." *US Department of State*, July 13, 2020. https://www.state.gov/u-s-position-on-maritime-claims-in-the-south-china-sea/.

Psaki, Jen. 2013. "Daily Press Briefing." *US Department of State*, December 9, 2013. https://2009-2017.state.gov/r/pa/prs/dpb/2013/12/218531.htm.

Quang, Nguyen Minh. 2019. "Saving the China-ASEAN South China Sea Code of Conduct." *The Diplomat,* June 29, 2019. https://thediplomat.com/2019/06/saving-the-china-asean-south-china-sea-code-of-conduct/.

Reagan, Ronald. 1983. "Statement by the President." March 10, 1983. https://www.gc.noaa.gov/documents/031083-reagan_ocean_policy.pdf.

Ross, Tommy. "Deterrence through Security Assistance: The South China Sea." *Parameters,* 47:4, Winter, 2017.

Roy, Denny. "Are US FONOPs Upholding Freedom or Stirring up Trouble?" *The Japan Times,* October 30, 2018. https://www.japantimes.co.jp/opinion/2018/10/30/commentary/world-commentary/u-s-fonops-upholding-freedom-stirring-trouble/#.XTjGGXt7mUk.

Rozman, Gilbert. 2011. "Chinese Strategic Thinking on Multilateral Regional Security in Northeast Asia." *Orbis* 55 (2): 298–313.

Reuters. 1974. "US Cautioned 7th Fleet to Shun Paracels Clash." *New York Times,* January 22, 1974. https://timesmachine.nytimes.com/timesmachine/1974/01/22/97464621.html?pageNumber=3.

———. 2017. "Delayed ASEAN Statement on S. China Sea Gives Beijing a Pass." *Business Insider,* April 29, 2017. https://www.businessinsider.com/r-asean-gives-beijing-a-pass-on-south-china-sea-dispute-cites-improving-cooperation-2017-4.

Schneider, Jacquelyn, and Julia Mcdonald. "The Role of Risk in Force Employment: A Tactical Level Analysis of Drone Weapon Use." Working Paper.

Schroeder, P.W. 1976. "Alliances, 1815–1945: Weapons of Power and Tools of Management." In *Historical Dimensions of National Security Problems.* Edited by Klaus Eugen Knorr. Lawrence: University Press of Kansas.

Seawright, Jason. 2016. *Multi-Method Social Science.* Cambridge, UK: Cambridge University Press.

Shugart, Commander Thomas. 2017. "Build All-UAV Carriers." *US Naval*

Institute Proceedings, September 2017. https://www.usni.org/maga zines/proceedings/2017/september/build-all-uav-carriers.

Skinner, B.F. 1938. *Behavior of Organisms.* New York: Appleton-Century-Crofts.

Slavin, Erik. 2016. "China Accuses US of Hypocrisy for Not Ratifying International Sea Law." *Stars and Stripes,* July 15, 2016. https://www. stripes.com/news/china-accuses-us-of-hypocrisy-for-not-ratifying-international-sea-law-1.419184.

Snow, Shawn. 2018. "The Corps Just Slapped a Counter-Drone System on an MRZR All-Terrain Vehicle." *Marine Times,* September 19, 2018. https://www.marinecorpstimes.com/news/2018/09/19/the-corps-just-slapped-a-counter-drone-system-on-an-mrzr-all-terrain-vehi cle/.

Stockholm International Peace Research Institute. "Military Expenditures Database." https://sipri.org/databases/milex. Last accessed Nov. 24, 2020.

———. "Sources and Methods." Section 5. https://www.sipri.org/data bases/milex/sources-and-methods#sipri-estimates-for-china. Last accessed Nov. 24, 2020.

Sullivan, Michael. 2016. "In South China Sea Dispute, Filipinos Say US Credibility is on the Line." *NPR,* July 17, 2016. https://www.npr. org/2016/07/17/486240079/in-south-china-sea-dispute-filipinos-say-u-s-credibility-is-on-the-line.

Thayer, Carlyle. 2013. "ASEAN, China and the Code of Conduct in the South China Sea." *SAIS Review of International Affairs* 33 (2).

United Nations. 1994. "Agreement Relating to the Implementation of Part XI of the United Nations Convention on the Law of the Sea." July 28, 1994. https://www.un.org/depts/los/convention_agreements/ texts/unclos/closindxAgree.htm.

US Department of Defense. 2015. "National Defense Authorization Act Asia-Pacific Maritime Security Strategy." https://dod.defense.gov/ Portals/1/Documents/pubs/NDAA%20A-P_Maritime_SecuritY_ Strategy-08142015-1300-FINALFORMAT.PDF.

————. 2018. "Assessment on US Defense Implications of China's Expanding Global Access." December 2018. https://media.defense.gov/2019/Jan/14/2002079292/-1/-1/1/EXPANDING-GLOBAL-ACCESS-REPORT-FINAL.PDF.

————. 2019. "Assessment on US Defense Implications of China's Expanding Global Access." December 2018. https://media.defense.gov/2019/Jan/14/2002079292/-1/-1/1/EXPANDING-GLOBAL-ACCESS-REPORT-FINAL.PDF.

————. 2020. "Military and Security Developments Involving the People's Republic of China, 2020." https://media.defense.gov/2020/Sep/01/2002488689/-1/-1/1/2020-DOD-CHINA-MILITARY-POWER-REPORT-FINAL.PDF.

US Department of State. 2010. "Daily Press Briefing, August 16, 2010." https://2009-2017.state.gov/r/pa/prs/dpb/2010/08/146001.htm.

USSOCOM. 2015. "The Gray Zone." White Paper. https://publicintelligence.net/ussocom-gray-zones/.

Valencia, Mark. 2017. "US FONOPs in the South China Sea: Intent, Effectiveness, and Necessity." *The Diplomat*, July 11, 2017. https://thediplomat.com/2017/07/us-fonops-in-the-south-china-sea-intent-effectiveness-and-necessity/.

Waltz, Kenneth N. 1979. *Theory of International Politics*. New York: McGraw-Hill.

Webster, Graham. 2015. "How China Maintains Strategic Ambiguity in the South China Sea." *The Diplomat*, October 29, 2015. https://thediplomat.com/2015/10/how-china-maintains-strategic-ambiguity-in-the-south-china-sea/.

Wilkins, Thomas. 2012. "Alignment, Not Alliance - The Shifting Paradigm of International Security Cooperation: Toward a Conceptual Taxonomy of Alignment." *Review of International Studies* 38 (1): 53–76.

Wong, Catherine. 2019. "'Divide and Conquer ASEAN': China Tries to Go One on One with Malaysia to Settle South China Sea Disputes." *South China Morning Post*, May 18, 2019. https://www.scmp.com/news/

china/diplomacy/article/3010790/divide-and-conquer-asean-china-tries-go-one-one-malaysia.

Wong, Chun Han. 2016. "Nine-Dash Line's Ambiguity a Good Thing, Argues Chinese Military Academic." *Wall Street Journal*, June 5, 2016. https://blogs.wsj.com/chinarealtime/2016/06/05/nine-dash-lines-ambiguity-a-good-thing-argues-chinese-military-academic/.

Wyne, Ali. 2016. "US Hypocrisy in the South China Sea." *Foreign Affairs*, July 14, 2016. https://www.foreignaffairs.com/articles/china/2016-07-14/us-hypocrisy-south-china-sea.

Yarhi-Milo, K. 2013. "Tying Hands behind Closed Doors: The Logic and Practice of Secret Reassurance." *Security Studies* 22 (3).

Yeo, Mike. "Testing the Waters: China's Maritime Militia Challenges Foreign Forces at Sea." *Defense News*, May 31, 2019. https://www.defensenews.com/global/asia-pacific/2019/05/31/testing-the-waters-chinas-maritime-militia-challenges-foreign-forces-at-sea/.

Zeng, Jinghan, and Shaun Breslin. 2016. "China's 'New Type of Great Power Relations': A G2 with Chinese Characteristics?" *International Affairs* 92 (4): 773–94. https://doi.org/10.1111/1468-2346.12656.

Zheng Zhi-Hua. 2015. "Why Does China's Maritime Claim Remain Ambiguous?" *Asia Maritime Transparency Initiative*, June 12, 2015. https://amti.csis.org/why-does-chinas-maritime-claim-remain-ambiguous/.

Made in the USA
Middletown, DE
23 March 2021